Read the Qur'an
Through 100 Verses

To my dear wife

The Prophet said,

*"Whoever recites one hundred
verses in one night*

*it will be as if he spent the night in
worship."*

[*Musnad, Ahmad Hanbal*]

Introduction

For better or for worse, the Qur'an is one of the most important books in the history of mankind. A quarter of humanity asserts that it contains the words of God Himself. Societies across a vast tract of the earth, stretching almost uninterrupted from the Atlantic coast of North Africa to the South Pacific cite it as their spiritual, moral, political and legal compass. Given current demographic trends and population movements, it seems inevitable that large urban areas in Western Europe will soon also turn Muslim majority. Yet astonishingly, despite the Qur'an's undoubted importance, barely any non-Muslims, and surprisingly few Muslims, have ever taken the time to actually read it.

In fairness, several factors make the Qur'an a difficult read. The text was composed in Arabic as rhyming verses to be memorised and recited and it loses this quality when translated and presented as printed prose. Stories within the Qur'an are usually only referred to briefly, or at best partially told, on the assumption that they would be well known by their audience: an assumption that does not apply to a modern readership. Many key Arabic words have no precise English equivalent, and some passages only make sense within a certain context, understood by Muslims in terms of the life of Mohammed as it is recorded elsewhere. All of this means that for a translated Qur'an to convey its meaning to the reader, the translator must either rewrite the text according to their own understanding of its purpose or else break it up with numerous explanatory footnotes and insertions.

However, the single most formidable obstacle to reading the Qur'an, and the one that this book is intended to help the Qur'an reader to overcome, is its lack of a clear chronological or thematic structure. It is not that the Qur'an lacks any structure at all. With familiarity, patterns can be discerned. After a short, introductory 'surah' (or chapter), surahs tend to be arranged according to the length of the surah, with the longest first, and verse lengths tend to decrease with the length of the surah. Surahs 2, 3, 4 and 5 tend to set out the Qur'an's message in contrast to Judaism and Christianity, whilst surahs 6, 7, 8 and 9 are presented as opposing those who commit the sin of '*shirk*' – the association of things with God (traditionally presented as polytheism and idolatry). Many of the shorter surahs have a symmetrical 'mirror' pattern with the second half revisiting the same themes encountered by the reader/listener in the first half but in reverse order, framing a pivotal middle section. Sometimes surahs seem to form clusters addressing related topics, and several surahs can be paired so that a theme that is central to one becomes the commencement and conclusion of its companion.

However, for those people seeking for themselves the answer to the question 'What does the Qur'an say?', either in general or in relation to a specific topic, the Qur'an's fragmentary structure is unhelpful. The purpose of this book is to offer navigational assistance to the new Qur'an reader who embarks upon that increasingly vital enquiry.

Paul Ellis

Paul Ellis is a retired barrister and teacher and a member of the National Committee of the For Britain Movement

Qur'an references appear in {__} brackets and, quotations, are, unless otherwise stated, taken from The Study Quran (2015).

References to related sections of this book appear in ⟨ ⟩ brackets.

Contents

Prologue: the bismillah

The numbered verses of each surah of the Qur'an, with the exception of **Surahs 1** and **9**, are preceded with the words of the bismillah, *'Bismillah al rahman al rahim'*:

> *In the Name of God,*
> *the Compassionate, the Merciful.*

In **Surah 1** the words of the bismillah are also the first words, but here they appear, not as a prelude to the body of the surah, but as its first verse, and the first verse of the Qur'an, {**1.1**}, ⟨**33.**⟩.

'Rahman' and *'rahim'* both derive from a common Arabic root *'r-h-m'* and are commonly translated as *'compassionate'* (alternatively *'gracious'* or *'beneficent'*) and *'merciful'* respectively. The word *'rahim'* was used by both Jews and Christians as an epithet of God in in pre-Islamic Arabia and derives from the Hebrew word *'ha-rahum'*. The bismillah is used as an invocation of God, prior to prayer, in a similar manner to that in which many Christians preface prayers by invoking the members of the Holy Trinity:

> *'In the name of the Father, the Son and the Holy Spirit'.*[1]

A comparison has also been drawn with a Zoroastrian text, *Dasatir I Asmai*, which begins each chapter:

> *'In the name of God,*
> *the Giver, the Forgiver, the Merciful, the Just'.*[2]

It is unclear if the bismillah, as an introduction to the surahs, was an original part of the Quranic text or a later addition. The fact that

Surah 1, of which it is effectively an abbreviation, is itself thought by some to be a later addition to the Qur'an supports the idea that it was added each surah as part of a late editing process.

Two, it is suggested equally plausible, theories have been proposed to explain why the bismillah is absent from **Surah 9**. One is that since **Surah 9** is generally considered to have been the last full surah to have been composed, the absence of the words may be a sign that the surah did not undergo some final editorial process prior to the Qur'an being canonised. Perhaps this was related to the death of Mohammed. The other possibility that has been suggested is that since **Surah 9** includes references to episodes in Mohammed's later military campaigns (see ⟨50.⟩ ⟨51.⟩ below), whilst his earlier campaigns are addressed in **Surah 8** (see ⟨39.⟩), it may have been the case that **Surahs 8** and **9** both once formed a single continuous text, which would have been the longest surah in the Qur'an, which may have been, at some stage, divided into two parts for convenience of recitation.

The words of the bismillah appear once in the Qur'an other than as the first words of a surah, as Solomon's greeting to the Queen of Sheba recounted in {27.30} see ⟨22.⟩

I

God and His Creation

1. God

Surah 2 (*al-Baqarah / The Cow*): 255

God, there is no god but He,
the Living, the Self-Subsisting.

Neither slumber overtakes Him nor sleep.

Unto Him belongs whatsoever is in the
heavens and whatsoever is on the earth.

Who is there who may intercede with Him
save by His leave? He knows that which is
before them and that which is behind them.
And they encompass nothing of His
Knowledge, save what He wills.

His Pedestal embraces the heavens and the
earth.

Protecting them tires Him not, and He is the
Exalted, the Magnificent.

[*The Study Quran, 2015, ed. Seyyed H. Nasr,
US-Iranian academic*]

God, in Islam as in all monotheistic religions, exists outside of creation: omniscient, omnipresent and omnipotent, the creator and sustainer of all that is and every individual's ultimate judge.

The Qur'an places a great emphasis upon the indivisible nature of God ('*tawhid*'). To associate anything with God is the sin of '*shirk*', regarded by many Muslims as the most grievous of all sins, that is said in {**4.48**} and {**4.116**} to be unforgiveable.

In particular the Qur'an condemns those who say that God has *'taken a child'* {**10.68**, **18.4**, **19.88**, **23.91**} - see also {**112.3**} - pointedly contrasting God's oneness in the Qur'an with the Christian doctrine of the Holy Trinity (see **(2.)** below), and *'the Jews* (who) *say Ezra is the son of God'* {**9.30**} (for whom there is no other historical record).

It also denounces those who claim that God has daughters ({**16.57**, **37.149**, **43.16**, **52.39**}), apparently refuting a belief that angels were God's daughters – rhetorically asking whether God would have chosen daughters over sons for Himself.

Seeking the intercession of saints as intermediaries between man and God is repeatedly dismissed as being of no assistance ({**2.48**, **2.123**, **32.4**, **39.44**, **74.48**}) although these apparently absolute statements are rendered equivocal by other verses that declare that effective intercessions is possible from angels {**40.7**} and a select few, *'those whom the Compassionate has granted leave and with whose word he is content'* {**20.109**}; similarly {**2.255**} above, {**21.28**, **34.23**} and {**53.26**}. Praying to saints is highly controversial in Islam, practised by some sufis but emphatically condemned by most Muslim schools as a form of shirk.

In the Qur'an, God uses *'al-lah'* (literally *'the god'*) as His personal name. Groups of verses frequently conclude with an attribute, or pair of attributes, of God, commonly called His *'beautiful names'* such as *'the Merciful, the Compassionate'* (see **_The bismillah_**) or *'the Exalted, the Magnificent'* at the conclusion of {**2.255**} above. Based upon a hadith[3] the Qur'an is commonly said to contain ninety-nine such beautiful names, and although there are many lists of ninety nine such names, none is definitive. In fact over two hundred such short descriptors of God have been identified within the Quran.[4] Some of these names describe essential aspects of monotheistic divinity (*'the Almighty'*, *'the Creator'*, *'the All-seeing, All-hearing'*). Through others, God provides mankind with suitably deferential terms to use when addressing Him ('*the Absolute Ruler*', '*the Pure One*', '*the Praiseworthy*', '*the Greatest*'). Yet more, such as '*the Kindly One*' and '*the Humiliator*', describe aspects of God's character – most commonly as either merciful or less so, depending upon the requirements of the context. {**59.23**} contains seven of these names:

> He is God other than Whom there is no god,
> the Sovereign, the Holy Peace, the Faithful,
> the Protector, the Mighty, the Compeller, the Proud.
> Glory be to Him above the partners they ascribe

Elsewhere, {**8.30**} offers a rare glimpse into God's thought process: '*They plotted, and God plotted. And God is the best of plotters.*' From a practical standpoint, these adjectives serve to divide the longer surahs into blocks of verses, and to round off a stanza with a rhetorical flourish.

Despite the strong cultural opposition in Islam to portraying God with human characteristics, the reference in {**2.255**} above to the heavens and earth as God's '*pedestal*' or footstool is merely one of several anthropomorphisms adopted to describe God within the Qur'an. After having created the heavens and the earth God is said, on seven occasions ({**7.54**}, see ⟨2.⟩, {**10.3**, **13.2**, **20.5**, **25.59**, **32.4**, **57.4**}) to have '*mounted His throne*'. God is said to have created Adam '*with (His) two hands*' {**38.75**} and to have kept the infant Moses {**20.39**}, Noah in his ark {**54.14**} and Mohammed {**52.48**}, '*under His (watchful) eye(s)*'. At the Last Day, ⟨96.⟩, all things will pass away '*save for His Face*' {**55.27**}, one of a dozen references to God's face including {**2.115**, **2.272**, **30.38**} and {**76.9**}; whereupon '*the whole earth shall be but a handful to him … and the heavens will be enfolded in his Right Hand*' {**39.67**}, and God will '*lay bare His shin*' towards which the people will prostrate themselves {**68.42**}.

2. God's Spirit

Surah 5 (*al Ma'idah/ The Table Spread*): 73

He sends the angels with the Spirit to carry His orders to whichever of His servants He wants so that they would warn people that He is the only God and that people must have fear of Him.

[Sarwar, 1981 (Pakistani-US, Shia)]

In Christian theology God comprises the Holy Trinity of God the Father, His Son Jesus (23.), and the Holy Spirit. The Qur'an twice rejects the concept of a trinity, at {5.73}:

> They certainly disbelieve who say 'Truly God is the third of three'.
>
> If they refrain not from what they say, a painful punishment will befall those among them who disbelieved.

and {4.171}: '*So believe in God and his Messengers and say not 'Three'. Refrain!*'

Yet, intriguingly, in {5.75} and {5.116} the Qur'an's author appears to have laboured under the misapprehension that Christians believe that the third member of the Trinity, after the Father and the Son - is Jesus's mother, Mary, rather than the Holy Spirit.

5.75:

The Messiah, son of Mary, was naught but a messenger ... and his mother was truthful.
Both of them ate food...

76. Say 'Do not worship apart from God...'

5.116:

O Jesus, son of Mary, did thou say unto mankind:
'Take me and my mother as gods apart from God'?

Yet despite the centrality to the Qur'an's message of the unicity of God, it is surprising to nevertheless find multiple references in the Qur'an to God's Spirit, the Holy Spirit and in one verse, {**26.192-3**}, the Trustworthy Spirit. These seem to contain an 'echo' of the Trinity.

In five places ({**16.2**, **17.85**, **40.15**, **42.52**, **97.4**}) the Qur'an describes God's Spirit as bringing down *'God's Command'*. This has led to some treating the term as an epithet for the angel Gabriel, **(9.)**, (whose name derives from the Hebrew *'gabri-el'* means *'strength of God'*). Gabriel is also generally held to be the *'Trustworthy Spirit'* of {**26.192-3**}. However, in each of {**16.2**, **70.4**, **78.38**} and {**97.4**}, though, a phrase such as *'the angels and the Spirit'* is used that would seem to unambiguously establish that the Spirit and angels in fact belong to two different orders of being.

Furthermore, Adam is said to have had *'life breathed into him of His (God's) Spirit'* ({**15.29**, **32.9**, **38.72**}) and in {**21.91**} and {**66.12**} exactly the same phrase is used to describe the conception of Jesus by the Virgin Mary. These two instances of the miraculous creation of human life one might have expected to lie within the power of God alone, rather than be delegated to an angel. If the *'breathing of God's Spirit'* into Adam and Mary might be regarded merely as merely an idiom to express God's ultimate responsibility for the giving of life, a different account of the conception of Jesus in {**19.17-20**} puts beyond any doubt that God's Spirit has its own persona, separate to God:

17. And she (Mary) veiled herself from them.
Then We sent unto her Our Spirit, and it assumed
for her the likeness of a perfect man.

18. She said 'I seek refuge from thee in the
Compassionate if you are reverent!'

19. He said 'I am but a messenger of thy Lord,
to bestow upon thee a pure boy.'

The phrase *'ruh al-qudus'* that is often translated using the familiar Christian term *'the Holy Spirit'*, appears in the Qur'an four times {**2.87**, **2,253**, **5.110**} and {**16.102**} and it can be no coincidence that three of these relate specifically to Jesus.

2.87 and **2.253**:

... And we gave Jesus son of Mary clear proofs and strengthened him with the Holy Spirit ...

5.110:

Then God will say 'O Jesus son of Mary, remember
... when I strengthened thee with the Holy Spirit ...'

It has been suggested that the verses referencing God's Spirit form part of an older corpus of verses within the Qur'an, written by a Christian sect, which were supplemented by later verses written from an entirely non-Christian perspective, see **⟨12. 'Muhammad'⟩** below. Be that as it may, during the time of Mohammed, some sought clarification of *'God's Spirit'*, although they are unlikely to have found the reply provided at {**17.85**} very enlightening.

They ask thee about the Spirit.
Say 'The Spirit is from the Command of my Lord,
and you have not been given knowledge,
save a little.'

A. The Cosmology of the Qur'an

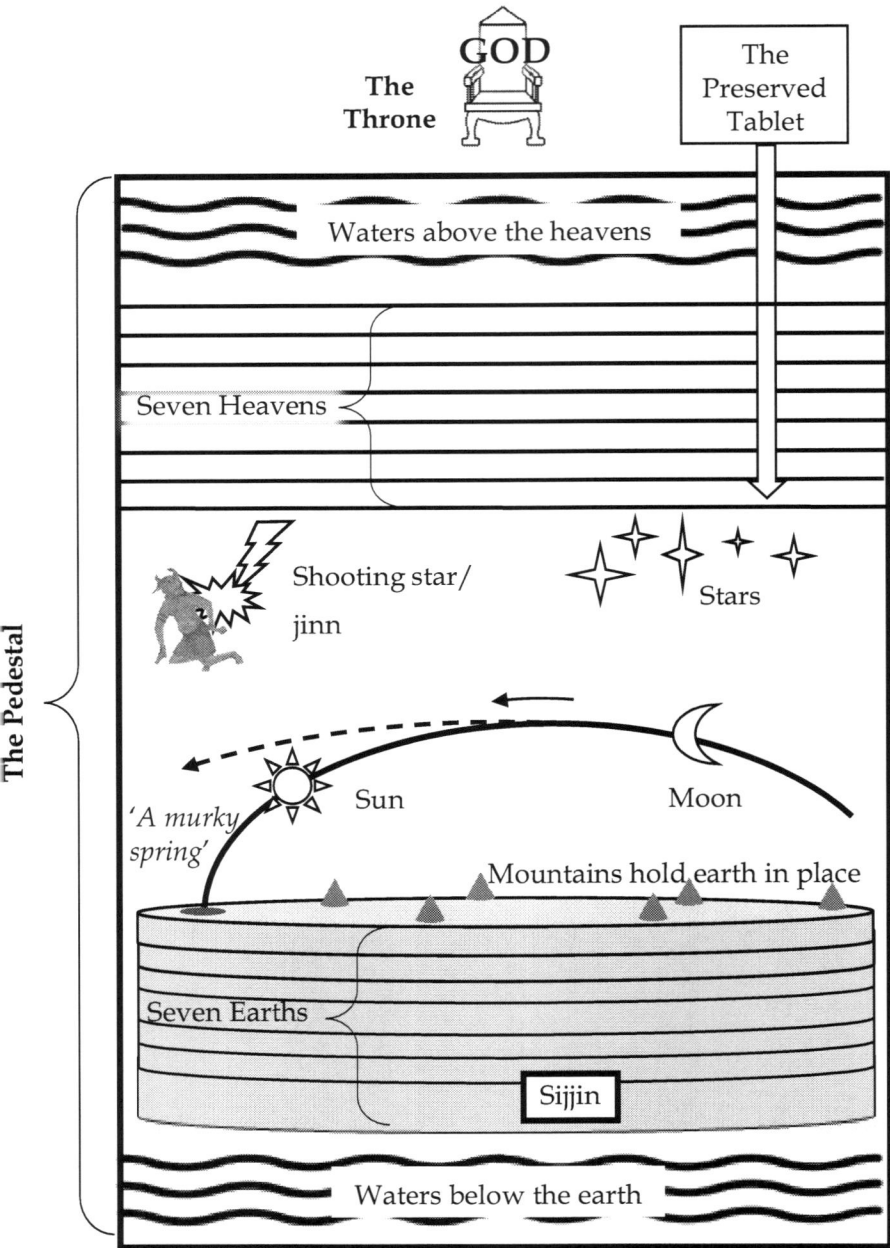

3. Creation
Surah 7 (*al-Araf/the Heights*): 54

Your Fosterer is certainly Allah,
Who created the skies and the earth in six
periods, then He set the balance on the
throne (of the universe).

He makes the night to cover the day,
which (i.e. the day) seeks the (night) rapidly
(in succession).

And the sun and the moon and the stars
are compelled to follow His command.

Is not His the creation and the command?

Blessed be Allah, the Fosterer of the worlds.

[*Mir Aneesuddin, 1993 (geologist, writer on Qur'an and science)*]

God's creation of '*the heavens and the earth*' is also described in
{**21.30-33, 41.11-12, 45.3-5, 50.38, 51.47, 57.4, 65.12**} and {**71.13-17**}.

In {**7.54**} above, and also in {**10.3, 11.7**} and {**25.59**} the Qur'an
describes God as having created the heavens and the earth in six
periods (in most translations rendered '*days*') following the well-
known account of creation in the Book of Genesis. By contrast, in
{**41.9-12**} three separate periods are described for the stages of
creation which aggregate to eight '*days*'. Although, following His
completion of creation, God is described as afterwards '*mounting
his throne*', see ⟨**1.**⟩ above, in {**50.38**} the Qur'an makes a point of
denying that He had been fatigued by the act of creation and
required rest. This insistence was likely to counter the popular
reading of Genesis 2.2: '*God rested on the seventh day*' that links the
seventh day to the Jewish institution of observing the sabbath.
Islam has no equivalent to the sabbath and in {**16.124**} the Jewish

sabbath is presented as a legal requirement imposed upon the Jews as a test or punishment for them, and for the breaking of which He turned some into apes, see ⟨87.⟩ below.

During Creation, the heavens and the earth were *'rent asunder'* {**21.30**}. The earth (in {**65.12**} described as though consisting of seven earths) is described as having been *'spread out'* {**15.19**, **20.53**, **43.10 50.7**} and {**51.48**}, some translations adding *'(like a carpet)'*, and fixed securely in place with mountains as *'stakes'*,{**78.7**}, *'lest it shake'*, {**16.15**, **21.30**}.

Above the earth, in {**41.12**, **65.12**, **67.3-4**} and {**71.15**}, God created the *'seven heavens'* - *'one upon the other'* {**67.4**, **71.15**} - in two days {**41.12**}. {**41.12**} also describes how God *'adorned the lowest heaven with lamps'* and a guard, and in {**71.15**} He *'made the moon a light therein and the sun a light'*. In these passages, the Qur'an partially adopts the cosmology of classical antiquity in which the earth lies below seven celestial domes which the sun, the moon and the five visible planets traverse with the lowest heaven being the setting of the fixed but moving array of stars. However the Qur'an does not make any connection between the seven heavens and celestial bodies, whilst the sun and moon are described as following arched paths - *'like a dried up palm stalk'*, {**36.39**} - and, in the case of the sun, descending each evening to earth, setting into *'a murky spring'*, see ⟨**30. Dhu'l Qarbnayn**⟩ below.

In {**15.16-18**, **37.6-10**} and {**72.8-9**} (see also {**67.5**}) the Qur'an asserts that meteors are missiles chasing away any jinn, see ⟨5.⟩, who attempt to listen to conversations or the recitation of the Qur'an in heaven.

15.16-18:

16. We have set constellations in the sky and we have adorned them for the onlookers.

17. And We have preserved them from every shaitan outcast [18.] save he who gains a hearing by stealth, and then a manifest flaming star pursues him.

4. Angels

Surah 35 (*Fatir/The Originator*): 1

All praise belongs to ALLAH,
the originator of the heavens and the earth,

Who employs the angels as Messengers,
having wings, two, three, and four.

HE adds to HIS creation whatever HE
pleases, for ALLAH has power over all
things.

[*Maulawi Sher Ali, 1969 (Ahmadiyya. The Ahmadiyya pursue a peaceful interpretation of the Qur'an given by Gulam Mirza Ahmad, 1835-1908. However, due to Ahmad's claims to prophetic authority, his teachings are treated as heretical within mainstream Islam.*]

Angels are said in hadith to be made from light.[5] They are always male, possibly on the basis that if they were female, they would not be qualified to act as witnesses, see ⟨81.⟩ below, the Qur'an rhetorically asking: '*Has he chosen daughters over sons? What ails you? How do you judge?*', {**37.150-154**}.

Six specific angels are referred to within the Qur'an:

- ❖ Gabriel (Jabril), whom Muslims believe to have transmitted the Qur'an to Mohammed (see ⟨9.⟩ below),

- ❖ Michael (Mikail), also ⟨9.⟩, who in Judeo-Christian tradition is the warrior angel, although, perhaps surprisingly, he is never invoked as such in relation to the Qur'an's many jihad verses (see **Part VIII** below),

- ❖ an unnamed angel who will blow the trumpet heralding the Last Day, {**6.73**, **39.68**}, see **(96.)** below, sometimes identified with the biblical archangel of healing, Raphael (Israfil),

- ❖ the Angel of Death, traditionally given the name of Azrael, who takes the souls of the departed to God {**32.11**}, and

- ❖ Harut and Marut, *'two angels of Babylon'* who appear, from their single reference in {**2.102**} to have been sent down by God in the time of Solomon **(22.)** to teach men magic as a trial, but who did not harm anyone thereby *'save with God's Leave'*.

In addition to these prominent angels, each person is said to be accompanied throughout their life by watcher angels:

82.10-12:

And yet truly over you there are guardians [11.] noble, writing [12.] knowing what you.

Further details of these angels are provided by {**43.80**} and {**50.18**} in the latter of which they are said to work in pairs *'seated on the right and on the left'*. In traditional Islamic angelology, the angel on the right records a person's virtuous deeds and exercises authority over the angel on the left who records sins.

Angels generally appear as sinless servants of God, but see **(7. *Iblis and al-Shaitan*)** below.

5. Jinn

Surah 72 (al-Jinn/The Jinn): 11

1. ... A band of jinn attentively listened to the recitation of the Qur'an and then (went back to their people) and said: ...

9. 'We would take up stations in the heaven to try to hear, but anyone who now attempts to listen finds a shooting meteor in wait for him.

10. We do not know whether evil is intended for those on the earth, or whether their Lord intends to direct them to the Right Way.

11. Some of us are upright and some of us are otherwise for we follow widely divergent paths' ...

[*Maududi, 1972 (Maududi was an Islamist and leading figure in the movement to establish Pakistan as an Islamic state)*]

Jinn are supernatural creatures, made from '*smokeless fire*', {**15.27**} and {**55.15**}, who are recognised in Islam as a lesser order of supernatural beings to angels, with greater freedom to be obedient or wayward. The word '*jinn*' is the source of the English word '*genie*', familiar to many from the *Tales of the Arabian Nights* genre, and especially the story of Aladdin.

{**72.1-11**} suggest that jinn can become believers by listening to the Qur'an, and some verses, such as {**55.33**} and {**6.130**}, are even addressed to '*men and jinn*'. Alternatively jinn may instead come to believe in error that God had a '*consort and child*' – a clear reference to the possibility that they may believe in Christianity. All of this shows that despite their supernature, jinn, like humans, are not naturally aware of the nature of God. As such they are also in jeopardy of being sent to Hell on the Last Day {**7.179**}.

The description of houris, see ⟨**99. Gardens of Paradise**⟩, as supernatural '*maidens of modest gaze, whom neither man not jinn has ever touched*' {**55.56**} implies that jinn have the desires and physical capacity for sexual intercourse.

Inevitably, there is a rich Islamic folklore concerning these impish figures, including a tradition that each person has a jinn assigned to them, alongside the two watcher angels, as a constant mischievous companion.[6]

See also ⟨**3. Creation**⟩ above and ⟨**22. Solomon**⟩ below.

6. Adam

Surah 23 (*al-Muminun*): 14

Then fashioned We the drop a clot,
then fashioned We the clot a little lump,
then fashioned We the little lump bones,
then clothed the bones with flesh,
and then produced it as another creation.

So blessed be Allah, the Best of creators!

[Pickthall, 1930 (British orientalist and convert)]

Humanity is said to have been created by God *'from a single soul'* ({**4.1**, **6.98**, **7.189**, **31.28**, **39.6**}), fashioned using as material either blood, {**96.2**} see **(32.)** below, water, {**25.54**}, clay, {**6.2**, **15.26-33**, **23.12**, **37.11**, **55.14**}, or dust {**30.20**}. God gave life to the first man by breathing into him *'of his Spirit'*, see **(2.)** above.

From this first human, a mate was created *'that he might find rest in her'* {**4.1**, **7.189**, **39.6**}, and from their loins proliferated many *'peoples and tribes'* {**49.13**} with *'diverse colours'* {**35.28**}.

Separately the Qur'an tells in several places, most fully at {**2.31-8**, **7.11-28**} and {**20.115-123**}, of the creation of the first man, Adam (Adem). It also describes the creation from him of an unnamed companion, in Islamic tradition called Hawa; both of them succumbing to the temptation of Shaitan to eat the fruit of a forbidden tree; their subsequent embarrassment at their nakedness prompting them to sew leaves together to make clothes, and their, and Shaitan's, expulsion from Paradise as a consequence of their disobedience. In these verses the Qur'an follows, in general terms, the narrative of Genesis chapter 3, although it should be noted that following the fall, unlike the biblical Adam and Eve, the Quranic Adam and his wife received words of comfort from God {**2.37**} and {**7.23-28**} that are understood as words of forgiveness, with the result that Muslim theologians have not developed from the story an equivalent to the Christian doctrine of original sin.

See also ⟨*7. Iblis/al-Shaitan*⟩ following.

7. Iblis and *al-Shaitan*

Surah 7 (*al-Araf/The heights*) 11

**And indeed, We created you,
then We fashioned you,
then We said to the angels
'Prostrate yourselves unto Adam.'**

**So they (all) did prostrate themselves except
Iblees; he was not of the prostrating ones.**

12. (He said) 'What prevented you that you
did not prostrate when I commanded you? '

He said ' I am better than him. You created
me of fire while You created him of clay. '

13. (Allah) said 'Get you down from this
(state). It does not befit you to behave
proudly therein. Therefore, go you out.
Verily you are of the abject ones'.

[*Sayyed Abbas Sadr-ameli, 2014, (Iranian Shia)*]

The refusal of Iblis to obey God's command to prostrate himself before Adam is also described at {**2.34**, **15.31-32**, **17.61**, **18.50**} and {**38.74-75**}. In {**7.11**} above Iblis is introduced as though he was one of the angels, despite his being *'made of fire'*, like a jinn, see **(5.)** above, rather than from light. In {**18.50**} he is described as being *'of the jinn'*.

In the role of the *'fallen angel'*, Iblis is often associated with the biblical figure of Satan. In the Qur'an *'al-Shaitan'* tempts Adam and his mate in Paradise by whispering suggestions that they eat from the tree that God had forbidden them {**7.20**} and {**20.120**}, see **(6. Adam)** above. However, elsewhere in the Qur'an, *'al-Shaitan'* tends to be used as a personification of the power of temptation, rather than an independent supernatural actor:

> 'Follow not the footsteps of Shaitan' {**2.168**, **2.208**, **6.142**} and {**24.21**},
>
> 'Shaitan promises naught but delusion' {**4.119-20**} and {**17.64**},
>
> 'No messenger or prophet did We send before thee but that when he had a longing, Shaitan would cast into his longing, whereupon God effaces what Shaitan cast' {**22.52-53**},
>
> 'Should a temptation from Shaitan provoke thee, seek refuge in God' {**41.36**},

or occasionally, when used in the plural form, as a class of creatures:

> 'We made for every prophet an enemy – shaitans from among mankind and jinn – who inspire each other with flowery discourse in order to deceive' {**6.112**},
>
> 'And among mankind are those who dispute concerning God without knowledge, and follow every defiant shaitan' {**22.3**}, and
>
> '(the stars are) a guard against every defiant shaitan' {**37.7**}, see ⟨**2. Creation**⟩ above.

For more references to al-Shaitan see {**2.268**, **7.27**, **17.53**, **35.6**, **36.60**} and {**59.16**}.

II

Islam

8. The Qur'an

Surah 25 (*al-Furqan/The Criterion*): 4

They say 'This is but a forgery which he (Muhammad) himself has concocted and certain other people have helped him in this.'

These people speak unjustly and lie.

They say 'These are legends of the earlier communities which he has got written down for himself and they are being dictated to him morning and evening.'

Say (O Muhammad) 'Rather He has sent it down Who knows the secrets of the heavens and the earth,

He is the Pardoning One, the Merciful One.'

And they say 'What a (queer) prophet! He eats food and goes about in the market place! Why has not an angel been sent down upon him so that he might be a co-warner with him? Or why has a treasure not been sent down upon him or (why has he not been given) a garden whose fruits he can eat?'

And the unjust ones say 'You (Muslims) are only following a victim of sorcery.'

[*Fazlur Rahman,1988 (from Major Themes of the Qu'ran)*]

The Qur'an literally means the '*recitation*'. Many verses (called '*ayah*', literally meaning '*signs*') are phrased as though addressed by God to His human interlocutor typically calling him '*O Prophet*' or '*O Messenger*', and preceding the substance of a revelation with a command to repeat what is about to be told. Over three hundred Quranic verses begin with the word '*Say…*' Occasionally, a verse rehearses a question that has been posed to Mohammed by his followers, commencing: '*They ask you concerning…*' This wording serves to make unambiguous the Qur'an's claim that it comprises, not merely inspired words from a human prophet, but the dictated words of God Himself, announced and recorded without human editing. This point is further emphasised on four occasions with the assertion that the Qur'an had been was '*sent down*' by God in Arabic {**12.2**, **16.103**, **26.195**, **41.3**}, an odd assurance for an rhyming recitation delivered in Arabic, and, one may suspect, an indication that some contemporary sceptics may have suspected that the Qur'an involved non-Arabic source material.

In {**85.22**} the Qur'an describes itself as having been inscribed upon a '*Preserved Tablet*', often understood by Muslims to mean that it is an uncreated scripture existing, like God, outside of time and space, possibly also referred to in {**56.77-80**} and {**80.11-16**}.

The Qur'an states that it was '*sent down*' within the month of Ramadan, {**2.185**}, on a particular '*blessed night*' {**44.2-3**}, probably connected with the Night of Power described in **Surah 97**, as a date in the calendar when each year the value of prayer will be increased one thousandfold. The apparent contradiction between the Qur'an's statement that it came down on a particular night and the accounts of its announcement by Mohammed over a period of twenty-two years is traditionally explained through the inference of an intermediate stage. The words of the Qur'an, it is speculated, must have been '*sent down*' from the Preserved Tablet, existing above the seven heavens, to the lowest heaven, see (**A. The cosmology of the Qur'an** and **3. Creation**) above, on the Night of Power, from which location it was revealed to Mohammed, verse by verse, over a period of twenty two years.

The Qur'an describes itself as *'clear'* to understand {**5.15**, **12.1**}, containing no discrepancies {**4.82**} (but see **(11. Abrogation)** below), *'easy upon thy tongue'* {**19.97**, **44.58**} and *'easy to remember'* {**Surah 54**: **17**, **22**, **32** and **40**}.

As evidence of its divine authorship, the Qur'an repeatedly lays down a challenge to its doubters {**2.23**, **4.82**, **10.38**, **11.13**, **17.88**} to produce verses of the same quality.

However, its claims to clarity contrast with verse {**3.7**} which accepts, possibly in response to questioning by Mohammed's followers, that in the interpretation of the Qur'an some verses should be read literally whilst others carry a hidden, more esoteric meaning:

> **3.7:**
>
> He it is Who has sent down the Book upon thee; therein are signs [*verses*] determined; they are the Mother of the Book and others symbolic.
>
> As for those whose hearts are given to swerving, they follow that of it which is symbolic, seeking temptation and seeking its interpretation.
>
> And none know its interpretation save God and those firmly rooted in knowledge.
>
> They say 'We believe in it, all is from our Lord' and none remember, save those who possess intellect.

The search for a hidden meaning within the Qur'an is a trait of Sufism – strongly disapproved of by many orthodox Muslims.

See also **(17. People of the Book)** below.

9. Gabriel

Surah 2 (*al-Baqarah / The Cow*): 97

Say 'Whoever is an enemy to *Jibriel* (Gabriel), for indeed he has delivered this (book) to your heart by Allah's permission, confirming as true what is in between its two hands (i.e. already there), and (it is) guidance and good news for the Believers.

98. Whoever is an enemy to Allah, and His angels and His Messengers and *Jibriel* and *Mikal*, then verily, Allah is enemy to the disbelievers.

[*Kamal Omar, 2003 (Quranicist: one who interprets the Qur'an without reference to the hadith)*]

Muslims believe that the words of the Qur'an were conveyed from God to Mohammed through the agency of the angel Gabriel (Jabril). The figure of Gabriel as the messenger angel is familiar to Christians through the gospels in which he is sent first to Zechariah to announce the forthcoming birth of John the Baptist (see Luke 1.11-12; a story told in the Qur'an at {**3.37-41**, **19.2-11**} and {**21.89-90**}) and then to Mary to announce her pregnancy with Jesus (Luke 26-38; Qur'an {**3.42-47**, **19.16-21**}). Gabriel also appears in the Hebrew Bible/Old Testament books of Daniel and Enoch.

The only verse of the Qur'an besides {**2.97**} above that mentions Gabriel's name is {**66.4**}, see ⟨**55.**⟩ below.

For the possible identification of Gabriel as the '*Trustworthy Spirit*' or '*God's Spirit*' see ⟨**2.**⟩ above; for angels generally see ⟨**4.**⟩ above.

10. The reliability of the recitation

Surah 53 (*al Najm/The Star*): 2

1. I swear, by the star when it goes down,

2. Your companion does not err, nor does he go astray.

3. Nor does he speak out of desire.

4. It is naught but revelation that is revealed, [5.] that the Lord of Mighty Power has taught him.

[Shakir, 1968 (Al Azhar Univ., Cairo, Shia-orientated)]

The words of the Qur'an, phrased as always in God's 'voice', reassure listeners that Mohammed, in reciting those words, has made no error. Further verses promise that God will protect the later transmission of the words:

15.9:

Truly it is We who have sent down the Reminder and surely we are its Preserver.

See also {**41.42**}.

Clearly there is a logical circularity in this guarantee of authenticity which can only be relied upon to the extent that it can itself be relied upon as authentic.

Several relatively minor variations in early Quranic manuscripts exist. A traditional Islamic explanation for these is that Mohammed taught his revelations to followers from different parts of Arabia in seven distinct dialects which were separately memorised and came to be written down in different ways, until the third caliph, Uthman, fixed the Qur'an's current standard canon ('the Uthmanic recension') and ordered that all variants be burned.

This explanation for the discrepancies in early Qur'an manuscripts, is doubted by most non-Muslim scholars, although an alternative explanation for the circumstances of its compilation and varied editions, has yet to gain an academic consensus.

11. Abrogation

Surah 2 (*al Baqarah/The Cow*): 106

Any message which We annul or consign to oblivion We replace with a better or a similar one.

Do you not know that Allah has the power to will anything?

[Al-Asi & Khan, 2008 (Institute of Contemporary Islamic Thought)]

Within the Qur'an, some verses clearly contradict one another. Examples include its teachings upon the sentence for fornicators, ⟨68.⟩, and the proper attitude to alcohol ⟨72.⟩. In {2.106}, and also in {16.101}, the Qur'an appears to explain such discrepancies by stating that one verse may replace or abrogate an instruction given in a previously announced verse.

Consequently, when applying any Quranic instruction, a Muslim must consider amongst other things whether it has been abrogated by a later instruction. Islamic scholars' opinions concerning the number of verses in the Qur'an that have been abrogated by later verses ranges from none to in excess of five hundred. In *Abrogation in the Koran*, by Rev. Anwarul Haqq a list of 252 verses that the author considers to have been abrogated is given.[7]

One of the factors complicating this issue is the fact that the verses in the Qur'an, as it was organised, it is said, by Uthman, are not ordered chronologically and there is no consensus either within or outside Islam as to the order in which verses were announced, or even whether each surah was announced as a single entity, or whether some later verses were inserted into existing surahs.

Traditionally surahs are classified either as Meccan, that is having been announced by Mohammed whilst he preached in Mecca to the predominantly pagan community of his home city, or as Medinan, announced by Mohammed after he had established his followers as a distinct community in Yathrib (later called Medina). Some typical features of Meccan and Medinan surahs are given below:

Typical features of Meccan surahs	Typical features of Medinan surahs
Surahs and individual verses tend to be shorter and more poetic.	Surahs and individual verses tend to be longer and more prosaic.
Tend to commence 'O people…'	Tend to commence: 'O you who believe…'
Content is more spiritual, i.e. more likely to address monotheistic worship, righteousness and personal virtue expressed in general terms, and supported by divine 'punishment narratives' (see ⟨18. Noah⟩ below) and graphic descriptions of heaven and hell.	Content is more practical, i.e. more likely to be concerned with obedience to 'God and His Messenger' (see 13. below), establishing laws and punishments (see Part VI Sharia) and exhortations to wage holy war (Part VIII Unbelievers).
'People of the Book' (see ⟨17.⟩ below) tend to be mentioned in a positive context; polytheists condemned.	Christians and Jews tend to be identified as such and denounced, along with 'hypocrites'.

Based upon their style and content, various proposals have been made for the order in which verses were announced. One such order is produced below:

The traditional order of the Qur'an surahs, as given in *The History of the Quran* by Allamah Abu Abd Allah al-Zanjan

Meccan	105	7	39	70	13
Verses	113	72	40	78	55
96	114	36	41	79	76
68	112	25	42	82	65
73	53	35	43	84	98
74	80	19	44	30	59
1	97	20	45	29	24
111	91	56	46	83	22
81	85	26	51		63
87	95	27	88	*Medinan*	58
92	106	28	18	*verses*	49
89	101	17	16	2	66
93	75	10	71	8	64
94	104	11	14	3	61
103	77	12	21	33	62
100	50	15	23	60	48
108	90	6	32	4	5
102	86	37	52	99	9
107	54	31	67	57	110
109	38	34	69	47	

Probably, the single most controversial area of Quranic interpretation is the degree to which the later, more bellicose Medinan verses (see ⟨38.⟩ ⟨53.⟩ and **Part VIII Unbelievers**) should be read as abrogating the more pacific and tolerant Meccan verses (such as ⟨35.⟩ ⟨45.⟩ and **Part VII Virtuous behaviour**).

12. 'Muhammad'

Surah 47 (*Muhammad*): 2

As for the believers who do good works and believe in what is sent down to Muhammad which is the truth from their Lord, He will acquit them of their sins and repair their condition.

[*Qaribullah, 2000, (Omdurman Islamic Univ., Sudan)*]

The word *'muhammad'* appears in four verses of the Qur'an: {**3.144**}, {**33.40**} see (*64.*), {**47.2**} above, and {**48.28**}. The word literally means *'he who is blessed'* or *'he who should be praised'* and is the active participle derived from the root word *h-m-d* or *'ahmad'* (*'bless'* / *'praise'*)which appears once in the Qur'an, {**61.6**}.

Some revisionist historians[8] have speculated that the word *'muhammad'* may not have originated as a personal name but as an honorific title. On this view the formal declaration of the Islamic faith, called the Shahada, which is normally translated as:

> *'There is no god but God*
> *and Muhammed is His Messenger'*

might have originally carried the meaning:

> *'There is no god but God*
> *and to be blessed is His Messenger'*

It has even been suggested that the title may originally have been adopted as a reference to Jesus. In *Early Islam, A Critical Reconstruction based Upon the Earliest Sources*, Karl-Heinz Ohlig proposes that within the four verses in which the word '*muhammad*' appears, two phrases - '*He has absolved them of their evil deeds*' in {**47.2**} above, and '*He is ... the seal of the prophets*' in {**33.40**} - link the word '*muhammad*' to concepts that seem to be more in keeping with a Christian than conventional Islamic theology.[9]

13. 'Islam'

Surah 3 (al-Imran/The House of Imran): 19

True Religion, in God's eyes, is islam (devotion to Him alone).

Those who were given the Scripture disagreed out of rivalry, only after they had been given knowledge - if anyone denies God's revelations, God is swift to take account.

[*Abdel-Haleem, 2004 (Al Azhar/Cambridge/SOAS, published in the Oxford World Classics series)*]

Both of the words *'islam'* meaning *'submission'* and *'muslim'* meaning *'one who submits'* derive from the word *'aslama'*: *'to surrender oneself'*, which shares the same *'s-l-m'* root as the word *'salaam'* (derived from the Hebrew word *'shalom'*) meaning *'peace'*. The word *'islam'* is on occasion used in the Qur'an in a way that is consistent with submission being the core principle of the faith:

'Enter into submission [islam] *all together...'* {**2.208**},

'Whosoever seeks a religion other than submission [islam] *it shall not be accepted ...* {**3.85**}, and

'What of one whose breast God has expanded for submission [islam]*...?* {**39.22**}.

See also {**5.3**, **6.125**, **9.74**, **61.7**} and ⟨77. *Dietary rules*⟩ below.

However, there is no record of the words *'Islam'* and *'Muslim'* being used as proper nouns relating to the religion based upon the Qur'an until over two centuries after the death of Mohammed.

14. Obedience to Mohammed

Surah 24 (*al Nur/Light*) 51

The only saying of the faithful believers, when they are called to Allah (His Words, the Qur'an) and His Messenger (SAW), to judge between them, is that they say 'We hear and we obey.'

And such are the prosperous ones (who will live forever in Paradise).

[*Hilali & Khan, 2005 (Wahabi/Saudi approved)*]

In the Qur'an the ideal of submission - see ⟨*13.*⟩ above - to God is achieved by adherence to the Sharia law and through obedience to God's messengers, of whom Muslims believe the most perfect to be Mohammed. {**24.63**} instructs the early believers: '*Do not deem the Messenger's calling among you to be like your calling to one another …*' and each of verses {**3.32**, **3.132**, **4.13**, **4.59**, **4.69**} and {**5.92**} employ the formula '*Obey God and obey the Messenger*' as though, for practical purposes, the two claims on a person's obedience were to be regarded as synonymous.

Similar requirements are found regarding the absolute duty to adhere to Mohammed's judgment in the arbitration of disputes in {<u>**Surah 4: 65**</u> and <u>**83**</u>} and (in a verse traditionally related to Mohammed's controversial marriage to Zeynab bint Jahsh, see ⟨*54.*⟩ and ⟨*64.*⟩ below) {**33.36**}.

15. Mohammed as *'a beautiful example'*

Surah 33 (*al Ahzab/The Parties*): 21

In truth, in (the sacred person of) Allah's Messenger (blessings and peace be upon him) there is for you a most perfect and beautiful model (of life) for every such person that expects and aspires to (meeting) Allah and the Last Day and remembers Allah abundantly.

[*Tahrir Ul-Qadri, 2012 (former Pakistani politician)*]

In this verse, God, speaking as always through Mohammed, extols his interlocutor as a *'beautiful example'* for believers to emulate. In {**68.4**} he is described as being *'of exalted character'*.

Mohammed's exceptionality is also evident in verses prescribing specific rules for Mohammed's domestic affairs: rules for his wives ⟨55.⟩ and visitors to his home ⟨56.⟩, and an exemption *'for thee alone, not for the rest of the believers'* from the Qur'an's marriage rules ⟨54.⟩.

In {**33.56**} believers are told to *'Invoke blessings upon him and greetings of the peace!'*: the basis of the Muslim custom of following any mention of Mohammed's name with a formula such as *'sallallahu alayhi wa-sallam'* (*'may Allah grant peace and blessings upon him'*) or simply *'peace be upon him'*.

However, determining the facts of the life of Mohammed for the purpose of using him as a moral exemplar is problematic. The first substantial biography of Mohammed, *Kitab al-maghazi* or *the Book of Expeditions*, often called *Sirat Rasul Allah* (*The Life of the Messenger of God*), written by Muhammad Ibn Ishaq was composed more than a century after Mohammed's supposed death and even this has now been lost in its original form, with extracts only preserved in work written after at least a further century had passed. Most of the *hadith* (short sayings of Mohammed's words and deeds based upon oral tradition) were committed to writing, assessed for reliability and collated into permanent collections from the ninth century onwards.

Both the biographies of Mohammed and the collections of *hadith* are conspicuous for describing Mohammed instructing his followers to commit acts that are reprehensible by modern ethical standards, such as brigandage (see ⟨*40. The raid at Naklah*⟩ and ⟨*41. The Battle of Badr*⟩ below), torture, the execution, enslavement and rape of captives (see ⟨*47. Banu Qurayza*⟩, ⟨*48. The Treaty of Hudaybiyya and promise of the spoils of Kaybah*⟩, ⟨*50. The Battle of Hunayn*⟩ and ⟨*67.*⟩). Mohammed is recorded as having personally kept slaves, including concubines, married two widows of men whom he had ordered killed, and, possibly most notoriously of all, undergoing a marriage ceremony with the six-year old daughter of his friend, see ⟨*59.*⟩

It is nowadays commonplace for Muslims faced with such accounts to dispute their accuracy, and virtually all secular scholars would agree that the existing sources for Mohammed's life should be treated as being of dubious historical reliability. However, there is no reason, based upon objective criteria, to reject as historically inaccurate only those stories of Mohammed that describe actions that contravene contemporary moral standards. Whilst the reliability of Mohammed's recorded life may certainly be challenged on historiographic grounds, so doing leaves contemporary Muslims with two problems. Without any reliable biography of Mohammed there is no narrative context in which many verses of the Qur'an can be understood, and the Qur'an's instruction to imitate Mohammed as a moral exemplar becomes impossible to follow.

16. Articles of faith

Surah 2 (*al-Baqarah / The Cow*): 285

285. The Messenger believes in what was sent down to him from his Lord, and the believers;

each one believes in God and His angels, and in His Books and His Messengers; we make no division between any one of His Messengers.

They say 'We hear, and obey. Our Lord, grant us Thy forgiveness; unto Thee is the homecoming'.

286. God charges no soul save to its capacity, standing to its account is what it has earned, and against its account what it has merited.

Our Lord, take us not to task if we forget, or make mistake.

Our Lord, charge us not with a load such as Thou didst lay upon those before us.

Our Lord, do Thou not burden us beyond what we have the strength to bear.

And pardon us, and forgive us, and have mercy on us, Thou art our Protector.

And help us against the people of the unbelievers.

[Arberry, 1955 (British orientalist; his translation considered by many to be the most elegant English translation of the Qur'an)]

These are the final verses of the Qur'an's longest surah and are often recited together.

{**2.285**} is often treated as a summary of Islam's essential articles of faith: namely monotheism, the existence of angels, see ⟨**4.**⟩ above, God's revelation to humanity through '*His Books and His messengers*', see ⟨**17.**⟩ following, and man's eventual judgment at the Last Day (see **Part X**).

{**2.286**} converts the creed into a prayer, seeking leniency and forgiveness, and culminating, in keeping with one of the most pervasive themes of the Qur'an, with an appeal for strength to prevail against unbelievers.

III

The People
of the
Book

17. People of the Book

Surah 3 (*al-Imran/ The house of Imran*): 3

**Step by step has He bestowed upon thee
from on high this divine writ, setting forth
the truth which confirms whatever there
still remains (of earlier revelations),
for it is He who has bestowed from on high
the Torah and the Gospel** [4.] aforetime, as a
guidance unto mankind, and it is He who has
bestowed (upon man) the standard by which
to discern the true from the false.

Behold, as for those who are bent on denying
God's messages - grievous suffering awaits
them.

For God is Almighty, an Avenger of evil.

[Muhammad Asad, 1980 (Austrian Jewish convert to Islam)]

The phrase '*People of the Book*' ('*ahl al-kitab*') is used frequently in the Qur'an as a collective term to refer to Jews, Christians (in the Qur'an, called '*Nasara*'), '*Sabians*' (who are referred to three times in the Qur'an, {2.62, 5.69} and {22.17}, and who are identified with the land of Sheba, but whose historical identity and religious beliefs remain uncertain), and '*Magians*' {22.17} (probably Zoroastrians).

The Qur'an refers to both the Torah and Injeel, which are together also referred to as '*the Book*', in {3.3} above, {3.48, 3.65, 5.46, 5.66-68, 5.110, 7.157, 9.111} and {48.29}. In addition, the Torah is mentioned on its own in {3.50, 3.93, 5.43, 61.6 and 62.4} and the Injeel, on its own, just once, in {57.27}.

The Torah (the books of Genesis, Exodus, Leviticus, Numbers and Deuteronomy) are sacred to Jews and Christians as the first five books of each of their respective bibles. The *'Injeel'*, usually translated as *'gospel'*, refers to the prophetic message of Jesus. It is notable that in the Qur'an the Injeel is always expressed in the singular, whereas Christianity recognises not one but four canonical gospels, each bearing the name of its putative human author. It is conceivable that the Injeel may, in fact, refer to none of the canonical gospels of the Bible, but to a Jewish-Christian 'Hebrew' gospel, see ⟨**23. Jesus**⟩ below.

{**3.3**} is one of numerous verses in which the Qur'an purports to confirm the Torah/Injeel, *'the Book that came before it'*, see {**Surah 2: 41, 89, 91, 97** and **101, 3.81, 5.48, 6.92, 35.31, 46.30**}. In the assertion in {**3.3**} above and many other places, that *'the Book'* had been as *'sent down'*, and references, {**5.46, 5.68**} to it having been *'given'* or *'taught'* by God to Jesus, the Qur'an depicts the Torah and Injeel as having originally consisted of direct messages sent from God to His prophets (although presumably not as part of the Preserved Tablet, see ⟨**8.**⟩ above). However, none of the books of the Torah nor any of the four New Testament gospels, could possibly support this interpretation.

It is likely that in some places the Qur'an is using *'the Book'*, in {**3.81**} *'a Book and Wisdom'* as a metaphor for an abstract idea (akin to the Christian concepts of *'the Word of God'* or *'the Good News'*) but in {**3.93**} the Qur'an says *'Say 'Bring the Torah and recite it...''* unambiguously envisaging it as a physical document.

The most common Muslim understanding is that whilst the original Torah and Injeel were scriptures that were, like the Qur'an, authored by God, their text and message had become corrupted by the rebellion and disbelief of Jews and Christians, who are denounced most comprehensively for this in {**Surah 5: 12-19, 41-86**, and **116-118**}.

The concept of 'the Book' is strong in the Qur'an, which, although it supposedly originally took the form of an oral recitation, occasionally describes itself as emanating from a 'book concealed', {**3.93**}, or 'the mother of the book' {**3.7**, **13.39**, **43.4**}. These terms are similar to the reference to the Qur'an as a Preserved Tablet, and are commonly deemed to refer to it in its intermediate state, lodged in the lowest heaven, awaiting revelation. The Qur'an is, of course, itself now generally encountered as a book, although in traditional Muslim belief, Mohammed's companions emphasised the virtue of reciting Mohammed's utterances from memory, see **(8.)** above.

B. Biblical Figures in the Qur'an

i. Simplified Genealogy of Genesis Figures

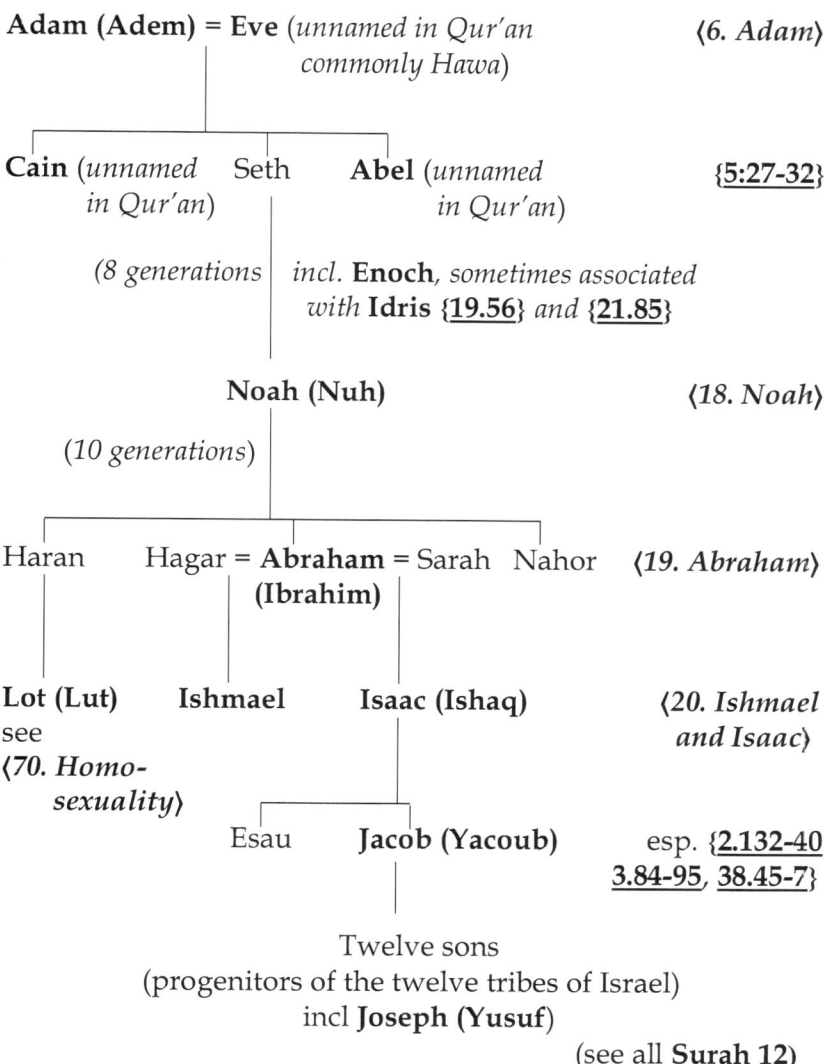

Adam (Adem) = Eve *(unnamed in Qur'an*   ⟨6. Adam⟩
                    commonly Hawa)

Cain *(unnamed*   Seth   Abel *(unnamed*   {5:27-32}
     in Qur'an)   *in Qur'an)*

          (8 generations incl. **Enoch***, sometimes associated*
                 with **Idris** *{19.56} and {21.85}*

Noah (Nuh)   ⟨18. Noah⟩

(10 generations)

Haran   Hagar = **Abraham** = Sarah   Nahor   ⟨19. Abraham⟩
                 (Ibrahim)

Lot (Lut)   Ishmael   Isaac (Ishaq)   ⟨20. Ishmael
see   and Isaac⟩
⟨70. Homo-
   sexuality⟩

         Esau   Jacob (Yacoub)   esp. {**2.132-40**
                                   3.84-95, 38.45-7}

Twelve sons
(progenitors of the twelve tribes of Israel)
incl **Joseph (Yusuf)**
(see all **Surah 12**)

ii. Context of Post-Genesis Biblical figures mentioned in the Qur'an

The Captivity in Egypt	In Genesis 46/{**12.99-101**}, Joseph brought all his family from Canaan to Egypt. Over subsequent generations their descendants, the Israelites, are said to have become slaves to the pharaohs.
The Exodus	**Moses (Musa)** and **Aaron (Harun)** led the Israelites to freedom **(21.)**
c.1050-c. 930 BC The Kingdom of Israel (the United Monarchy)	**Samuel** (*unnamed in Qur'an*) anointed the first two kings of Israel {**2.246-251**}: **King Saul (Talut)** and **King David (Dawood)** {**21.78-80**, **27.15-16**, **34.10-13**, **38.17-29**} The third King of Israel was David's son **Solomon (Suleiman) (22.)** After c. 930 BC the kingdom divided into Israel and Judah.
c.597-539 BC The Babylonian Captivity	In 597 Judah was conquered by the kingdom of Babylon which held prominent Jews hostage in Mesopotamia. The Babylonian Captivity was the setting in which several major Jewish prophets including Ezekiel, Isaiah, Jeremiah, Elijah (the **Elias/Ilyas** of {**6.85**, **37.123-132**}), **Elisha**, {**6.86**, **38.48**}, and **Ezra** (see **(1.)**) emerged.

539-333 BC Judea as part of the Achaemenid Empire	In 539, Babylon was defeated by the Achaemenid emperor, Cyrus the Great who ended the Jewish Captivity but kept Judah under Achaemenid control.
333-140 BC The Hellenic Period	The Achaemenids were defeated in 333 BC by **Alexander the Great**, who appears in the Qur'an as *Dhu'l Qarnayn* ⟨30.⟩ Judea remained under the control of the successor (Ptolemaic and Seleucid) empires to Alexander's realm until 140 BC.
140-37 BC The Hasmonean Kingdom	The Maccabean Rebellion (140 BC) re-established Israel as an independent kingdom.
From 37 BC Roman rule	In 37 BC, the Roman Empire imposed Herod the Great as a proxy king over Judea, then annexed it as a Roman province in AD 6, during the infancy of **Jesus (Isa) ⟨23.⟩**.

Jonah (Yunus or **Dhu'l Nun/** *'the Man of the Fish'*):
{**10.98-9**, **21.87-88**, **37.139-48** and **68.48-50**}

and

Job (Ayyub) {**21.83-84** and **38.41-48**}

cannot be placed within a historical context, each of their
stories originating in the Bible's Wisdom literature.

18. Noah

Surah 7 (*al-Araf/The Heights*): 59

59. Of old, sent We Noah to his people,
and he said 'O my people! worship God.
Ye have no God but Him. Indeed. I fear for
you the chastisement of the Great Day'...

64. Marvel ye that a Warning should come to
you from your Lord through one of
yourselves, that he may warn you, and that
ye may fear for yourselves, and that haply ye
may find mercy?

[*Rodwell, 1861 (British clergyman)*]

In the Book of Genesis (chapters 6-9) God warns Noah of an imminent flood and instructs him to build an ark to save himself and two of every type of creature: a male and a female.

A Mesopotamian clay tablet deciphered in 1873 demonstrates that the biblical account of the flood is a variation of an episode forming part of an Assyrian saga, the Epic of Gilgamesh. It seems likely that during the Babylonian Captivity this pagan legend was adopted by the captive Israelites and adapted to monotheism as an allegory for God's punishment and mercy.

Many of the Qur'an's references to prophets from the Bible and Arabian folklore focus upon God's punishment of those who reject their instructions. This 'punishment narrative' motif is repeated frequently throughout the Qur'an, often with little more than the names of the prophets and the nature of the punishment changing. The rhetorical advantages of this theme to a preacher attempting to incentivise his audience to follow him is obvious.

In the Qur'an, the story of Noah is summarised seven times, {**7.59-64**, **10.71-74**, **11.25-49**, **23.23-31**, **26.105-122**, **54.9-17**} and {**71.1-28**}. In each one of these passages the focus of the story is placed firmly upon the punishment having been earned by Noah's people for their having ignored their prophet's warnings and mocked him. The ark's famous animal passengers are mentioned – briefly - in only two of the seven accounts. The prominent application of the punishment motif to Noah's story is particularly notable, however, since in the biblical version Noah makes no attempt to warn anyone of the impending flood at all.

19. Abraham

Surah 3 (*al Imran/The House of Imran*): 96

Indeed, the first house to be set up for mankind is the one at Bakkah, blessed and a guidance for all nations.

97. In it are manifest signs (and) Abraham's Station, and whoever enters it shall be secure.

And it is the duty of mankind toward Allah to make pilgrimage to the House — for those who can afford the journey to it — and should anyone renege (on his obligation).

Allah is indeed without need of the creatures.

[Ali Quli Qara'i, 2005]

In the Book of Genesis (chapters 12-18) Abraham, then an old man and childless, is said to have formed a covenant with God in which God promised him a land for his descendants who would be as numerous as the stars in the night sky. Thereafter, Abraham begat two children. His first-born son was Ishmael, his child by Hagar, the servant of his wife, Sarah. Later, Sarah also bore Abraham a son, Isaac, after which, Sarah persuaded Abraham to send Hagar and Ishmael away.

The Qur'an contains many references to Abraham (Ibrahim) recounting his discovery of monotheism by reflecting upon the movement of the stars, moon and sun {**6.74-83**} and his rebellion against his idolatrous father (including {**19.52-67**, **21.52-67**, **26.69-82**} and {**37.83-96**}), neither of which story is found in the Bible;[10] his visitation by angels, {**11.69-76**, **15.51-61**, **51.24-34**}, and his willingness to sacrifice his son on God's command, see **(20.)** below.

In {**3.96**} above, Abraham, in {**2.125-127**} together with his elder son, Ishmael (see also {**14.35-9**}), is said to have built '*the first house established for mankind*', alongside which to settle his progeny.

In Islamic tradition, this house is traditionally associated with the Ka'aba, the rectangular shrine in Mecca, and its description in the Qur'an as '*the first house*' is explained by the creation of a further tradition that the Ka'aba stands where Adam and Eve first lived after their expulsion from Eden.

However, the Qur'an offers no explanation as to how or why Abraham and Ismael might have come to Mecca, a thousand miles from the Chaldees (north-west of modern Kuwait) and Canaan, where Abraham is said in the Bible, to have lived (see 〈*31. Mecca*〉 below).

The last words of {**3.97**} '*Pilgrimage to this house is a duty upon mankind before God for those who can find a way*', is the basis of the religious duty on Muslims to make the hajj pilgrimage to Mecca once in their life if this is possible (see *E. **The Five Pillars of Islam**, below).

20. Isaac and Ishmael

Surah 37 (*al-Saffa/Those arranged in ranks*): 102

101. We gave him (Abraham) glad tidings,
the glad news of the birth of a forbearing son.

**102. When his son was old enough to work
with him, he said 'My son, I have had a
dream that I must sacrifice you. What do
you think of this?'**

**He replied 'Father, fulfil whatever you are
commanded to do and you will find me
patient, by the will of God'.**

[*Sarwar, 1981, see* ⟨2.⟩]

This is a version of the biblical story (told in Genesis 22) in which God commanded Abraham to sacrifice his infant son Isaac as a test of his devotion. Only after Abraham had demonstrated his willingness to make the sacrifice that God had commanded, did God order that Isaac be replaced with an animal. In the Qur'an the working age and compliant '*gentle son*' whom Abraham dreamed he must sacrifice is unnamed and Muslim scholars tend to identify him not with Abraham's younger son Isaac (in the Quran, Ishaq), but with his elder half-brother, Ishmael,[11] from whom Mohammed's tribe, along with many Arabs, claimed descent.[12]

Muslims commemorate this episode during the festival of Eid al Adha ('*feast of sacrifice*'), held at the conclusion of the traditional time for the hajj pilgrimage (see ⟨8.⟩ above). In this festival the slaughtering of animals plays a central role.

21. Moses

Surah 17 (*al-Isra/The Night Journey*): 102

101. We gave Moses nine self-evident signs.

So, ask the Children of Israel (to tell you what happened) when Moses came to them (appealing to Pharaoh on their behalf) and Pharaoh responded to him: 'Truly, Moses, I think you are engaged in witchcraft.'

102 And (Moses) answered 'You know very well that no one but the Lord of heavens and earth can produce such miracles as evidence so that you may see. So, Pharaoh, (since you have chosen rather to reject what you see) I know you are utterly lost.'

103. And then Pharaoh wanted to wipe (the Children of Israel) from the face of the earth, and We subsequently caused Pharaoh and all who joined him to drown.

[*Kaskas & Hungerford, 2016*]

The Book of Exodus tells of Moses leading the Israelites out of slavery in Egypt and of their wandering in the wilderness of Sinai for forty years. According to Exodus, the infant Moses had been saved from a massacre of Hebrew children through the actions of his sister, Miriam, who placed him in a basket amongst the reeds on a section of river-bank frequented by the pharaoh's daughters, by one of whom he was discovered and adopted. Moses was raised in the royal court but was forced to flee Egypt after killing a slave driver for beating an Israelite. He later returned to demand freedom for his people, a demand that was eventually granted after God smote the Egyptians with a series of plagues.

After the pharaoh had emancipated the Israelites, Moses led them out of Egypt, through a miraculously parted Red Sea. During the following forty years he is described leading the often rebellious Israelites in Sinai, during which time he proclaimed a large number of strict religious laws, including the Ten Commandments, carved by God upon tablets of stone.

Moses (Musa) is named one hundred and forty-three times in the Qur'an, more than any other person, and Muslims see the life of Mohammed as having closer parallels with that of Moses than that of any other prophet.

Moses, like Mohammed, is said to have been raised as an orphan {20.37-40}, to have preached monotheism to a disbelieving and hostile audience {10.75-95, 20.43-60, 43.46-56} and {44.17-24} and to have led his people from persecution into wilderness (including {7.136-8, 26.52-56, 44.23-31}). Moses' preaching to the court of the pharaoh is the pre-eminent 'punishment narrative' Quranic motif (see ⟨18. Noah⟩ above), illustrated by {17.101-103} above which refers to the account in Exodus of Pharaoh's charioteers drowning in the Red Sea as they attempt to recapture the fleeing Israelites. Oddly, although the Qur'an in {17.103} depicts Pharaoh as having drowned with his army, but elsewhere it states that he was saved from drowning as a sign for others {10.93}.

The most important attribute shared by Moses in the Bible and Mohammed in Islam is the role adopted by each of them as the proclaimer of God's law and as its supreme judge. In the Qur'an, as in the Bible, Moses is described, most fully at {20.11-24}, receiving laws directly from God and conveying them to the Israelites on 'tablets' {7.145} - a clear reference to the Ten Commandments.

In all these roles – prophet, leader and lawgiver - Moses is presented as a forerunner of Mohammed, and the Ten Commandments as a prototype of the Qur'an's Preserved Tablet.

An enigmatic allusion to Moses in the Qur'an appears in the story recounted at {**2.67-72**}, from which **Surah 2** (*'The Cow'*) takes its name. This passage, the meaning of which is unintelligible from the text of the Qur'an alone, links a divine instruction to slaughter a yellow or red cow with the successful investigation of an unexplained death. The best explanation of this cryptic passage appears to be that the Qur'an has conflated two separate sacrifice rituals prescribed in the Torah (Numbers 19.1-3 and Deuteronomy 21.1-8), adding a new, miraculous, element that, when these rituals were conducted by Moses, a murder victim was resurrected to name his killer.[13]

A young Moses also features in the unfamiliar role of a disciple, in the story of Al-Khidr **(29.)**

22. Solomon

Surah 27 (*al-Naml*/*The Ants*): 18

18. When they came to the Valley of the Ants, an ant said 'Go into your dwellings, ants, lest Solomon and his warriors should unwittingly crush you.'

19. (Solomon) smiled, laughing at her words, and said 'Inspire me, Lord, to render thanks for the favours with which You have favoured me and my parents, and to do good works that will please You.

Admit me, through Your mercy, among Your righteous servants.'

[*Dawood, 1954 (commissioned by Penguin Classic as first popular translation of the Qur'an)*]

In the Hebrew Bible Solomon is the third king of Israel and is particularly renowned for his wisdom. The treatment of Solomon in the Qur'an is more innovative and fantastical than that of any other biblical prophet, with the possible exception of Moses' following of Al Khidr, (see ⟨29.⟩ below).

{27.15-45} recounts how Solomon could communicate with animals, and '*gathered … his hosts of jinn* (see ⟨5.⟩ above), *men and birds marshalled in ordered ranks*' {27.17}. He understood and smiled when he heard one ant (as he passed through the '*Valley of the Ants*') warn its fellow ants of Solomon's army's approach.

The story proceeds to tell of Solomon learning from a late-arriving hoopoe bird of its discovery of the land of Sheba ruled over by a queen. Solomon sends the hoopoe bird back to Sheba with a letter inviting the queen to visit him and worship God, which she does (a retelling of the visit of the Queen of Sheba to Solomon that is described in the Bible in 1 Kings 10 and 2 Chronicles 9).

Both the conclusion of {**27.15-45**}, in which the Queen of Sheba attempts to paddle in a crystal floor, having mistaken it as a pool of water (based upon a variation of the biblical story contained in a rabbinic commentary) and a separate story {**38.30-40**} in which God places a corpse upon Solomon's throne, could fairly be said to have tested the powers of Quranic interpreters to find their intended purpose.

In {**34.14**} Solomon makes a group of jinn labour for him as a punishment, but whilst he is overseeing them Solomon dies leaning upon his staff, so that his workforce toil on, unaware of their taskmaster's death. The jinn only discover that Solomon has died when a termite eats through his staff causing it to break and his body to fall:

34.14:

... And when he fell down, the jinn saw clearly that, had they known the Unseen, they would not have tarried in humiliating punishment.

23. Jesus

Surah 4 (*al Nisa/Women*): 157

156. ...(A)nd for their (*the Jews'*) misbelief,

and for their saying about Mary a mighty calumny,

[157] and for their saying 'Verily, we have killed the Messiah, Jesus the son of Mary, the apostle of God'....

But they did not kill him, and they did not crucify him, but a similitude was made for them.

And verily, those who differ about him are in doubt concerning him; they have no knowledge concerning him, but only follow an opinion.

They did not kill him, for sure!

[*Palmer, 1880*]

Christians regard Jesus as God incarnate, His *'Word made flesh'* (John 1.14), who as the promised Messiah brought about, through his death and resurrection, a new covenant between man and God based upon man's redemption from sin. Although Jesus and his followers were all Jews, and Jesus is recorded in the gospels as presenting his mission as the fulfilment of Hebrew prophecies, his message was inclusive and attracted many early non-Jewish converts. The Council of Jerusalem, c. AD 50, attended by Saints Peter and Paul (The Acts of the Apostles, chapter 15), decided that gentile Christians should not be considered generally bound by the Mosaic law and from this time Christianity has developed as a religion distinct from Judaism. A number of Jewish-Christian sects, such as the Nazarenes and the Ebionites, are, however, known to have existed as recently as Mohammed's time, who accepted Jesus as the Jewish Messiah but denied his divinity and rejected the writings of St Paul, and who instead continued to follow the Mosaic law.

Jesus (Isa) is an important figure in the Qur'an, regarded as second only to Mohammed, referred to frequently and with both his mother (the only female to be named in the Qur'an), and his supposed maternal grandfather having surahs named after them.

The Qur'an accords with many Christian beliefs concerning Jesus. It agrees with the gospels that Jesus was born of a virgin, {**3.47**, **19.21**}, performed miracles ('*thou wouldst heal the blind and the leper by My Leave and thou wouldst bring forth the dead by My Leave*', {**5.110**} (see also ⟨**25.**⟩ below), and received a divine revelation, the '*Injeel*' (see ⟨**17.**⟩ above). The Qur'an describes Jesus eight times ({**3.45**, **4.171-2**, **5.17**, **5.72**, **5.75**, **9.30-31**}) as the Messiah, at least twice, {**3.45**} and {**4.171**}, as the Word of God (also possibly at {**19.34**}), and in {**4.171**}, he appears even to be equated with '*a Spirit from God*' (see ⟨**2. God's Spirit**⟩ above): '*Verily the Messiah, Jesus son of Mary, was only a messenger of God, and his Word which he committed to Mary, and a Spirit from him.*'

The Qur'an also, surprisingly, associates Jesus with the phenomenon of the Holy Spirit, ⟨**2.**⟩, and incorporates Jesus in the anticipated events leading up to the Last Day, ⟨**96.**⟩, when he shall return to earth to herald the imminent judgment of God ('*he is indeed a portent of the Hour*' {**43.61**}).

In {**4.157**} above, though, the Qur'an rejects Jesus's death by crucifixion. The most common explanation offered in Islam for God's statement that He had made it appear to the Jews that they had killed Jesus is that God substituted some other person to be crucified in Jesus's place. No reason is suggested for such a deception. Rather, than being raised from the grave, Islamic tradition, based upon {**3.55**}, recalls that Jesus was taken up to heaven before any earthly death - although this account conflicts with Jesus's own prediction of his death and resurrection as recounted in {**19.30-33**}.

Most importantly, the Qur'an utterly rejects, including at {**4.171**} and {**Surah 5: 17, 72-77** and **116-8**, **9.30-31**, **17.111**, **19.34-38**, **43.57-59**, **112.1-4**}, the Christian belief that Jesus is the Son of God:

> <u>5.72</u>
>
> They certainly disbelieve those who say
> 'Truly God is the Messiah, the son of Mary'...
>
> Surely whoever ascribes partners unto God,
> God has forbidden him the Garden, and his refuge
> shall be the Fire.
>
> And the wrongdoers shall have no shelter.

In this, the Qur'an reflects the Christology of the Jewish-Christian sects, referred to above. These sects are known to have compiled several 'Hebrew gospels'. All of these are now lost other than for short excerpts, quoted by the church fathers (always referring to them in the singular as *'the Hebrew gospel'*) in order to condemn them for their heresy. According to the hadith accounts, the second person whom Mohammed told about his revelations was his wife, Khadija's, cousin, Waraqa bin Nawfal *'who, during the Pre-Islamic Period became a Christian and used to write the writing with Hebrew letters. He would write from the Gospel in Hebrew as much as Allah wished him to write.'*[14] There has long been academic speculation that the Qur'an's view of Jesus and Christianity was primarily formed by a Jewish-Christian tradition rather than the prevailing Trinitarian Christianity.[15]

Despite the frequent and reverential references to the figure of Jesus in the text of the Qur'an, the only words attributed to Jesus are those said to have been spoken by him as an infant {**19.30-33**}. However, in {**7.40**}, the author of the Qur'an borrows Jesus's distinctive phrase from Matthew 19.24:[16]

7.40:

Truly those who deny Our signs and wax arrogantly against them, the gates of Heaven shall not be opened for them, nor shall they enter the garden till the camel passes through the eye of the needle.

This do we recompense the guilty!

It is noteworthy that in {**7.40**} above the barrier to salvation is changed from worldy attachment to denial of God's '*signs*' (i.e. the verses of the Qur'an).

Elsewhere, Jesus's parables of the sower (Matthew 13.1-23) and the mustard seed (Matthew 13.31-2) no doubt provide the inspiration for the Qur'an's {**2.261-265**} and {**31.16**} respectively.

Although the Qur'an contains verses referring to God's mercy, see ⟨*97. Judgment*⟩ below, the Qur'an's prevailing regime of religious laws enforced with harsh punishments (see **Part VI Sharia**) and frequently repeated expressions of separation and hostility to unbelievers (see **Part VIII Unbelievers**) displays a fundamentally different approach to morality to Jesus's complete rejection of violence, instruction of universal and encouragement to selfless compassion and the unconditional forgiveness of enemies.

24. Discrepancies between the Bible and the Qur'an

Surah 3 (*al Imran/The House of Imran*): 35

(Remember) when Imran's wife said
'God, I pledge dedication of what is in my
womb to You, so accept it from me, indeed
You hear all and know all'.

[*Ali Bakhtiari Nejad (Iranian, Shia)*]

On two occasions the Qur'an appears to confuse Mary ('*Maryam*') the mother of Jesus with Miriam the elder sister of Moses and Aaron. In {19.28} Mary is addressed by her people as '*sister of Aaron*' and in {3.35} Mary's father (who is unnamed in the New Testament but in Christian tradition is known as Joachim) is given the name of Imran, a name that is too similar to that of Amran, the biblical father of Miriam, Moses and Aaron, for the Maryam/Miriam confusion not to be confirmed. This is a spectacular error, since the most rudimentary familiarity with the Bible should have told the author of these verses that Moses must have lived many centuries before Jesus.

Other likely instances of errors over biblical stories include:

- {2.249} which describes Saul instructing his soldiers not to lap water straight from a stream, a version of a biblical story involving Gideon (Judges 7.5); and

- {28.3} in which a servant of pharaoh is named Haman, the same name as a servant of Ahasuerus, king of Persia in the Book of Esther.

25. Apocryphal sources

Surah 5 (*al Ma'idah/ The Table Spread*): 110

> When God will say: 'O Jesus son of Mary,
> recall My favor upon you and upon your
> mother, how I supported you with the Holy
> Spirit. You spoke to the people from the
> crib, and in maturity. How I taught you the
> Scripture and wisdom, and the Torah and
> the Gospel.
>
> And recall that you molded from clay the
> shape of a bird, by My leave, and then you
> breathed into it, and it became a bird, by
> My leave.
>
> And you healed the blind and the leprous,
> by My leave,
>
> and you revived the dead, by My leave.
>
> And recall that I restrained the Children of
> Israel from you when you brought them the
> clear miracles.
>
> But those who disbelieved among them
> said `This is nothing but obvious sorcery'.

[*Itani, 2009 (Lebanese-US)*]

The Qur'an retells biblical stories with many details that appear to have their origin in Talmudic (Jewish) commentaries or early Christian devotional writing. Many of these allusions are identified *The Bible and the Quran* by Gabriel Said Reynolds.

For example {**5.110**} refers to a supposed miracle performed by Jesus as a child that is told in the apocryphal *Infancy Gospel of*

Thomas. In this story, Jesus is chided by his father, Joseph, for making clay birds on the sabbath, but removes the evidence of his having done so by breathing life into the birds so that they fly away.

The two other miracles involving Jesus that are recounted in the Qur'an - a palm tree that offered its fruit to Mary and a spring that appeared at her feet, both at the command of the new-born infant Jesus, both at {19.24} - are clearly variants of a tradition recorded in the apocryphal *Infancy Gospel of Matthew*, although the latter places these miracles as having occurred during the Holy Family's flight to Egypt.

Other instances of the Qur'an apparently adopting non-biblical sources include:

{5.31} A raven demonstrating to Cain how to bury his brother's body contained in the second century collection of Rabbinic commentaries of Pirque Eliezer ben Hyrcanus,

{12.26-28} Joseph's innocence of adultery with Potiphar's wife having been proved by the fact that his tunic had been torn from behind, an added detail to the biblical story of Joseph provided by the fifth century homilies of Narsai,

{12.67} Jacob's instruction to Joseph's brothers, on their return to Egypt with Benjamin, to enter Pharaoh's court by different gates, taken from a Talmudic commentary, Genesis Rabbah, written between 300-500,

and

the hostility of angels to the creation of Adam, see (**6. Iblis and al-Shaitan above**), recounted in the Babylonian Talmud Sanhedrin (3rd – 5th centuries) and also in the sixth century Syriac Christian text, *The Cave of Treasures*.

Yet more examples are given in:

⟨19 *Abraham*⟩ (note 10),

⟨28. *The sleepers in the cave*⟩,

⟨28. *'Al-Khidr'*⟩,

⟨30. *Dhu'l Qarnayn*⟩ and

⟨74.-75. *'Spreading corruption in the land'*⟩.

IV
Non-biblical stories

26. The Arab prophets

Surah 9 (*al-Tawbah/Repentence*): 70

Did the news not come to them of those
before them, the people of Noah and 'Aad
and Thamud, and the people of Abraham,
and the dwellers of Median, and those
overthrown?

Their messengers came to them with clarity.
It was not God who wronged them, but it
was themselves that they wronged.

[*The Monotheist Group, 2011 (multi-denominational)*]

The Qur'an refers many times, and especially in **surahs 7, 11** and
26 to three Arab prophets whose stories closely fit the 'punishment
narrative' motif described in **(*18. Noah*)** above.

Hud, see especially {**7.65-72, 11.50-60, 26.123-139, 46.21-26**} and
{**54.18-21**}, preached monotheism to the people of Ad, '*vice regents
after the people of Noah*' {**7.69**}, but when his message was ignored
their cities were destroyed by a great storm: '*a cloud bound for their
valleys... a wind carrying a painful punishment destroying everything by
the Command of its Lord*' {**46.24-25**}.

Saleh, see especially {**7.73-79, 11.61-68, 15.80-84**} and {**26.141-158**},
preached to the people of Thamud who had been '*made vice regents
after Ad*' {**7.74**}, who are also associated with the people of Al Hijr
referred to in {**15.80-84**}. God had granted them a giant she-camel
as a blessing and as a test of their obedience to His command not
to harm it, but when the Thamud hamstrung her, '*the earthquake
seized them and morning found them lying lifeless in their abode*' {**7.78**}.

Shuaib, preached to a people at Midian, {**7.85-91**, **11.84-94**} and {**23.20**}, also referred to as '*the people of the thicket*' or '*the people of the wood*', {**15.78**, **26.176-189**, **38.13**, **50.14**}, whom he condemned for giving false measure (see ⟨*82. **Honesty***⟩). They were destroyed by a great earthquake, that is described in {**7.91**} using the same words as those used to describe the destruction of the people of Thamud in {**7.78**}.

Shuaib is sometimes associated with Jethro, the father in law of Moses, who is described in Exodus 3.1 as '*the priest of Midian.*'

The consistency of the theme is summed up in {**7.94**}:

> We sent no prophet to a town but that We seized its people with misfortune and hardship that haply they would humble themselves...
>
> 98. Did the people of the towns feel secure from Our Might coming upon them in broad daylight while they were playing?
>
> 99. Did they feel secure from God's plotting? None feels secure from God's plotting save the people who are losers.

A further non-biblical prophet, Luqman, is quoted in {**31.12-19**} giving words of counsel to his son.

27. The elephant

Surah 105 (*al-Fil/ The Elephant*): 1

Have you not considered how your Lord dealt with the People of the Elephant (the army of Abrahah, the viceroy of the Negus, king of Abyssinia, at Yeman)?

2. Did He not (cause the war to end in confusion and) ruin their plan (to destroy Ka`bah by making it revert on themselves)?

3. And He sent against them flocks of birds, [4] (which tore off flesh from their bodies to eat, by) striking against them stones of hardened and petrified clay.

5. And thus He reduced them to rotten chaff (and in a similar way will they be ruined who would ever make an attack to destroy Ka`bah).

[*Amatul Rahman Omar and Abdul Omar, 1990 (a married couple, making this the first English translation of the Qur'an by a woman)*]

The Qur'an here refers to the story of Abraha, '*the viceroy of the negus, king of Abyssinia*'. Abraha is a historical figure who is known to have led an expedition from the East African kingdom of Aksum to protect the Christian minority in Yemen, from persecution. This persecution is thought to have included the immolation of the '*people of the ditch*' described in the Qur'an's **Surah 85**.

Abraha established a Christian kingdom in Yemen, but there is no evidence that he ever pushed as far north as Mecca, nor that his army on the Arabian Peninsula included an elephant. According to a story recorded by Ibn Ishaq, Mohammed's grandfather had been instrumental in organising the evacuation of Mecca in advance of Abraha's army. The story proceeds to record how, as the Meccans looked down on their city from surrounding hills:

> *God sent upon* (the invaders) *birds of the sea like swallows and starlings. Each bird carried three stones, like peas and lentils, one in its beak and two between its claws. Everyone who was hit died but not all were hit. They withdrew in flight by the way they came…*[17]

28. The sleepers in the cave
Surah 18 (*al-Kahf/The Cave*): 12

10. A group of young (Christian) men resolved to escape persecution; they betook themselves to the Cave - in a mountain nearby - where they expressed their invocatory prayer.

'O Allah, our Creator', they prayed, 'extend to us of Your Mercy, what will help us endure our tribulation, and direct us to a course of action determining what You commend for us of future events'.

11. We, in response, struck them deaf and induced them to sleep for a number of years.

12. Then We roused them and provoked them to activity so that We would see which of the two arguing parties would come closer to the exact length of time they remained dormant, as a marvel of Allah correlative with Resurrection.

[*Al-Muntakhab, 1985*]

This story is a variation on a Christian legend, the *Seven Sleepers of Ephesus*, recorded by Jacob of Sereugh (450-521) in which Christian youths fleeing persecution by the Roman Emperor Decius (249-51), 'slept' in a cave, miraculously awakening over a century later to discover to their amazement that whilst they had slept the empire had become Christianised. The Qur'an's account of the story even includes a reference to the sleepers having money, a detail that is irrelevant to the Qur'an's narrative, but which in Jacob of Sereugh's account provides the evidence – in the form of Decius' head on the coins - as to how long the youths had been sleeping.

29. 'Al Khidr'

Surah 18 (*al-Kahf/The Cave*): 81

74. So they (*the Servant of God and Moses*) journeyed on till when they met a young boy. He (*the Servant of God*) slew him.

Moses said `What! hast thou slain an innocent person without his having slain anyone! Surely, thou hast done a hideous thing!'...

[*The Servant of God later explains his actions to Moses, referring to his victim's parents*]

81. 'So we desired that their Lord should give them in exchange one better than he in purity and closer in filial affection.'

[*Maulawi Sher Ali, see* ⟨4.⟩]

In {18:65-82} the Qur'an tells a story in which a young Moses, (see ⟨21.⟩ above) follows a mysterious unnamed '*servant of God*', traditionally called '*Al Khidr*' and associated with the colour green.

The Servant of God permits Moses to travel with him on the condition that Moses does not question his actions, but despite having agreeing to this term, Moses cannot resist asking Al Kihdr for explanations when the latter scuttles a ship, kills a boy and builds a wall, all for no apparent reason.

At the conclusion of the account, Al Khidr explains the reasons for his actions, which in all three cases involves his knowledge of some hidden or future circumstance that Moses could not possibly have known.

The story of 'Al-Khidr' clearly derives from a text attributed to John Moschus (d. 619) in which an angel teaches a monk about wisdom by killing a boy and building a wall, later offering explanations that are almost identical to those offered in similar circumstances by the Qur'an's Servant of God.

The tale is clearly an allegory, intended to instruct faith and obedience. However, Al Khidr's explanation for having killed the boy in {**18.74**}, which was that the boy's death was in order to prevent him growing up to challenge his parents with '*rebellion and disbelief*', appears to justify the taking of a life in circumstances that today would lead to it being referred to as an 'honour killing'.

30. Dhu'l Qarnayn

Surah 18 (*al-Kahf/The Cave*): 94

94. 'Dhu'l Qarnayn,' they said, 'Gog and Magog are ravaging this land. May we pay you a tribute so that you erect a barrier between us and them?'

95. He answered 'That with which my Lord has established me is better (than any tribute). Hence, do but help me with strength, and I shall erect a rampart between you and them!

96. Bring me blocks of iron!' At length, when he had filled up the gap between the two mountainsides, he said 'Ply your bellows!'

Then, when he made (the iron glow like) fire, he said 'Bring me molten copper which I will pour over it.'

97. And thus their enemies were unable to scale (the rampart), nor could they dig their way through it.

98. He said 'This is a mercy from my Lord. Yet when the time appointed by my Lord shall come, He will make this (rampart) level with the ground.

My Lord's promise always comes true.'

[Sayyid Qutb, 1965 (Egyptian Islamist, leading figure in the Muslim Brotherhood, executed 1966)]

Dhu'l Qarnayn – literally *'the two horned one'* - is generally accepted to be a legendary depiction of Alexander the Great, who was sometimes referred to as *'the two horned one'* in pre-Islamic epics. Alexander's appearance in the Qur'an, {**18.83-98**}, is anomalous, since he is not an obviously religious figure.

In the Legend of Alexander the Great, written by Syriac Chrsitains at about the same time as the traditional life of Mohammed, Alexander reaches a place that might be described as the ends of the earth, and describes a place where the sun rises, burning anyone nearby. In {**18.86**} Dhu'l Qarnayn is described reaching *'the place of the setting sun'* which he discovered to be a *'murky'* or *'muddy'*, sometimes *'warm'*, spring. Within its literary context, {**18.86**} clearly recounts that at sunset the sun descends from the sky to the earth at a particular place, and sinks into a *'murky spring'*, an idea that is also referenced at {**36.38**}, although the rather more mundane interpretation is now sometimes offered that Alexander may merely have reached a western coastline and observed a sunset over water.

A more dramatic story involving Dhu'l Qarnayn relates to his imprisonment of Gog and Magog (in Arabic, Ya'juj and Ma'juj), told at {**18.92-97**}. The names of Gog and Magog first appear in the Book of Ezekiel chapters 38 and 39 in which the prophet Ezekiel foretells that shortly before the End of Days, Israel will face an invasion by the people of Magog, led by King Gog. In later Jewish apocalyptic literature this feared invasion became associated with two separate peoples, the people of Gog and the people of Magog, who also appear as two peoples in the principal Christian apocalypse, the Book of Revelation (20.8).

So far as it is known, it was the first century Jewish-Roman historian Josephus who first linked the tribes of Gog and Magog to the legends of Alexander the Great.[18] In later, but still pre-Islamic, fantastical versions of his life, Alexander is said to have built a great gate of iron and brass across a valley to keep Gog and Magog from breaking through and attacking a tribe that had sought his help (*Legends of Alexander the Great*).

After the completion of the Qur'an, the characteristics of Gog and Magog continued to be embellished. The Jewish Encyclopaedia summarises their description in post-Quranic Arab literature thus:

> *They are of small stature attaining to only one half the size of a man. Very ferocious they have claws instead of nails, teeth like a lion, jaws like a camel and hair which completely hides their bodies. Their ears, hairy on one side, are so large that they use one for a bed and the other for a covering.*

See ⟨*96. The Last Day*⟩ below.

V

The Life of Mohammed

B The Traditional Chronology of the Life of Mohammed

Year (AD)	Event	See below
570	Birth of Mohammed	
595	Mohammed's marriage to Khadija	
610	Mohammed announces the first Qur'an revelation ⟨32.⟩	
	Mohammed preaches in Mecca	⟨33. The Salat⟩
		⟨34. Mohammed's family⟩
		⟨35. 'To you your religion and to me mine'⟩
619	Death of Khadija	
621	The Isra/Night Journey to the 'farthest Mosque' ⟨36.⟩	⟨37. Splitting the moon⟩
622	The Hijra: Mohammed migrates to Yathrib/Medina	⟨38. The first permission to fight⟩ ⟨39.⟩
623	Raid on Naklah ⟨40.⟩	
624	Battle of Badr ⟨41., 42.⟩	⟨43. Changing the Qiblah⟩
625	Battle of Uhud ⟨44.⟩	

⟨45. 'No compulsion in religion'⟩

627   Battle of the Trench **⟨46.⟩**

Massacre/enslavement of the Banu Qurayza **⟨47.⟩**

628   Treaty of Hudaybiyyah

629   Siege of Kaybar

⟨48.⟩

630   Conquest of Mecca **⟨49.⟩**

Battles of Hunayn, Autas **⟨50.⟩**

631   Conquest of Tabouk **⟨51.⟩**
Raids into Yemen
Farewell Sermon

⟨52. 'The Sword Verse'⟩

⟨53. Jizya⟩

632   Death of Mohammed

31. Mecca and Yathrib

Surah 48 (*al-Fath/Victory*): 24

It is He who restrained their hands from
you, and your hands from them, in the
hollow of Mecca, after that He made you
victors over them.

God sees the things you do.

[*Arberry, see* (**16.**)]

It is clear from its text that much of the Qur'an was composed
during an ongoing conflict that it addresses repeatedly. This
conflict appears to have involved two settlements. One is
described as a religious sanctuary and centre of pilgrimage,
referred to by terms such as '*Al Masjid al Haram*' (literally the
'*forbidden*' or '*sacrosanct*' '*place of prostration*'), including at {**Surah 2:
141-50, 191 and 217**}, {**9.19**} and {**17.1**}, and the '*Mother of all Cities*'
{**6.92**, **42.7**}. The other settlement is mostly described simply as '*al-
madinah*' ('*the city*'), for example in {**Surah 9: 101 and 120**}, {**33.60**}
and {**Surah 22: 26 and 29**}.

In the traditional understanding of the life of Mohammed, the
sanctuary is Mecca, and the city, present day Medina, then called
Yathrib. The names Mecca and Medina each appear in the Qur'an
just once: Mecca in {**48.24**} above, within the context of the signing
of the Treaty of Hudaybiyyah (see (**48.**) below), and Yathrib in
{**33.13**}.

In Islamic tradition Mecca, is also identified with the place where:

- Adam and Eve first lived after their expulsion from
  Paradise (**16**),

- Hagar and Ishmael made their home after leaving Abraham, and

- Abraham and Ishmael built the Ka'aba,

see ⟨*19. Abraham*⟩ above.

Since the 1970s revisionist historians have pointed out that despite the centrality of Mecca to the story of Islam and the duty on all Muslims to make pilgrimage to Mecca if they are able to do so, and the vast Islamic empire that was said to have been created by the followers of Mohammed within a few decades of his death, there is no reliable historical or archaeological evidence at all for the existence of Mecca prior to 741, over a century after the death of Mohammed. Moreover, accounts of Mohammed's life, such as grazing livestock as a young man, are inconsistent with Mecca's harsh desert climate. This has led some, to question whether the events of Mohammed's life, if they took place at all, in fact occurred elsewhere and were later transposed to Mecca.[19]

32. The first revelation

Surah 96 (*al-Alaq/The Blood Clot*): 1

1. Recite, in the name of thy Lord,

Who [2.] hath created all things, who hath created man of congealed blood.

3. Recite, by thy most beneficent Lord,

4. Who taught the use of the pen,

5. Who teacheth man that which he knoweth not.

[George Sale, 1734 (first accurate English translation)]

These are traditionally regarded in Islam as the first verses of the Qur'an to have been announced by Mohammed.

33. The Salat

Surah 1 (*al-Fatihah/The Opening*): 1

In the Name of Allah, the Mercy-Giving, the Merciful,

2. All praise is due to Allah (alone) the Sustainer of all the worlds,

3. The Most Gracious, the Most Merciful.

4. Lord of the Day of Judgement!

5. You alone do we conform to; and unto You alone do we turn for help.

6. Show us the straight way, [7.] The way of those on whom Thou hast bestowed Thy Grace, those whose (portion) is not wrath, and who go not astray.

[*Al Asi & Khan, see* ⟨**11.**⟩]

Since surahs are ordered in such a way that they tend to decrease in length throughout the Qur'an, the existence of one of the shortest surahs as the first verse shows that it was positioned there to act as an introductory prayer. The suggestion has been made that the first and last two surahs of the Qur'an were likely later added to a previously existing body of text as *'framing texts'*, [20] a suggestion strengthened by an account that all three verses were said to be absent from a Qur'an compiled by one of Mohammed's companions.

See also ⟨**7. Prologue: the bismillah**⟩ above.

This, the first verse of the canonical Qur'an, is said to have been called by Mohammed the 'mother' or 'essence' of the Qur'an. It is recited by Muslims before they perform each *rak'a* (prostration) of their *salat*: the obligatory Muslim five-daily prayers (see **E. The Five Pillars of Islam**, below).

It has been suggested that the structure of {**1.1**} copies that of the Lord's Prayer of Christianity (Matthew 6.9, Luke 11.2):[21]

1. Praise of God:

    'Hallowed be thy name'   *'All praise is due to Allah'*

2. Anticipation of the Last Day:

    'Thy Kingdom come, Thy Will be done on earth as it is in heaven'   *'Lord of the Day of Judgment'*

3. Appeal for practical sustenance:

    'Give us this day our daily bread'   *'Unto you alone do we turn for help'*

4. Appeal for moral guidance:

    'Lead us not into temptation, but deliver us from evil'   *'Show us the straight way... the way of ... those who do not go astray'*

There is no single place in the Qur'an where it is stated that a Muslim should pray five times a day. The standard Muslim cycle of five daily prayers at: dawn ('al-fajr'), noon ('al-zuhr'), late afternoon ('al-asr'), sunset ('al-maghrib'), and the early hours of the night ('al-isha') has presumably been constructed from reading together several verses.

{**6.52**, **24.58**} and {**40.55**} anticipate only two formal prayer times: at, or shortly before or after, the rising and setting of the sun. Other verses {**11.114**, **17.78-79**, **20.130**, **50.39-40**} also refer to praying '*at the ends of the day*', {**20.130**}, but in addition recommend praying during the night. {**11.114**} specifies '*the early hours of the night*', but in the other verses the time of the night prayers is not fixed and {**17.78-79**} is explicit that nocturnal praying is recommended but not a strict obligation. One verse {**30.17-18**} instructs believers to give glory to God at four times, referring specifically to noon and the late afternoon in addition to dawn and dusk:

> 17. ... when you enter upon the evening and when you rise at morn.

> 18. His is the praise in the heavens and on the earth when the sun declines and when you reach the noontide.

Finally, {**2.238**} refers to a '*middle prayer*', anticipating an odd number of prayers. Consequently, it would seem likely to suppose, the early night became a fifth mandatory prayer time.[22]

The account of Mohammed's negotiations with God on the number of prayers, see ⟨**36. The Night Journey**⟩ below, is clearly a much later pious invention.

34. Mohammed's family

Surah 111 (*al-Masad/The Palm Fibre*): 1

May the power (the hands) of Abu Lahab perish! He will perish.

2. Neither his wealth nor what he has earned has helped him.

3. He will be pushed down into a flaming Fire

[4.] and (so will) his wife, the wood-carrier.

5. She will have a rope of rough palm leaves around her neck.

[Haneef, 2017]

According to the traditional narrative, Mohammed was born after the death of his father and was raised by his mother; then, upon her death, by his grandfather and finally by one of his seven uncles, Abu Talib. Abu Talib did not convert to Islam but two of Mohammed's other uncles – al-Abbas and Hamza - did.

A further uncle, Abu Lahab (literally *'father of the flame'*: probably an epithet marking him out for condemnation rather than a personal name), is said to have become one of the leaders of the opposition to Mohammed's movement in Mecca. For this rejection, a whole surah, **111**, of the Qur'an was dedicated to his denunciation, proclaiming to its audience that God had cursed him to burn in the hellfire and that God would cause his wife, who by her actions had effectively added fuel to her husband's pyre, to be hung. To increase the impact of this threat, God is even recorded as having specified the precise material from which the noose by which He would hang her, would be made.

35. 'To you your religion, and to me mine'
Surah 109 (*al-Kafir/ the Disbelievers*): 6

1. Say 'O disbelievers!

2. I worship not that which ye worship.

3. Nor worship ye that which I worship.

4. And I shall not worship that which ye worship.

5. Nor will ye worship that which I worship.

6. Unto you your religion, and unto me my religion.'

[*Pickthall, see* ⟨6.⟩]

According to Ibn Ishaq, the above verses were revealed about a group of people from Mohammed's tribe who had made an attempt to engage in dialogue with him, suggesting:

Come follow our religion and we will follow yours. You worship our idols for a year and we worship you Allah the following year. In this way, if what you have brought us is better than what we have, we would partake of it and take our share of goodness from it; and if what we have is better than what you have brought, you would partake of it and take your share of goodness from it'.

(Mohammed) *said: 'Allah forbid that I associate anything with Him', and so Allah, exalted is He, revealed* {**109.1-6**}. *The Messenger of Allah, Allah bless him and give him peace, then went to the Sacred Sanctuary, which was full of people, and recited to them the Surah. It was at that point that they despaired of him.*[23]

See also **Part VIII Unbelievers**, below.

36. The Night Journey

Surah 17 (*al-Isra/The Night Journey*): 1

Immaculate is He who carried His servant on a journey by night from the Sacred Mosque to the Farthest Mosque, whose environs We have blessed, that We might show him some of Our signs.

Indeed, He is the All-hearing, the All-seeing.

[*Ali Qarai, see* ⟨**19.**⟩]

Based upon several accounts received by Ibn Ishaq, this brief passage in the Qur'an is treated by Muslims as referring to an episode in which God took Mohammed overnight on a supernatural winged horse called Buraq from Mecca to Jerusalem ('*the furthest mosque*').

According to one of the accounts told to Ibn Ishaq, on his arrival at Jerusalem, Mohammed found Abraham, Moses and Jesus gathered to meet with him. According to another, better known, account Mohammed ascended from Jerusalem through the seven heavens, (see ⟨**3.**⟩ above) meeting as he passed through the different levels: Adam, Jesus and John the Baptist, Joseph son of Jacob, Idris (possibly the biblical prophet Enoch), Aaron, Moses and Abraham. As he began his descent to earth, Moses encouraged Mohammed to repeatedly return to God to intercede with Him to reduce the required number of daily prayers from fifty, in stages, down to five.

In 692 a shrine, the Dome of the Rock, was built on Temple Mount in Jerusalem at the point from which Muslims now believe

Mohammed ascended. The Al Aqsa ('*farthest*') Mosque was later built nearby.

The story of the night journey has now become the basis of the claim that is often made that Jerusalem, and in particular the precinct of the Dome of the Rock and Al Aqsa Mosque, is the third most holy place in Islam, a claim that is a major factor in the ongoing Arab-Israeli conflict. However, it will be noted that {**17.1**} makes no reference to Jerusalem, which is nowhere named in the Qur'an, nor to Mohammed's ascension to heaven, surely the most important and striking element of the story as it later came to be told. In fact, the identification of Jerusalem as the site of the '*furthest mosque*' ('*masjid*', or '*place of prostration*') in {**17.1**} is poorly supported, since no place of worship in the religious tradition established by Mohammed was built in Jerusalem in Mohammed's lifetime, and there is no other obvious category of place for which Jerusalem would have been farthest from Mecca.

37. Splitting the Moon

Surah 54 (*al-Qamar/The Moon*): 1

The Hour (of doom) is drawing near,
and the moon has split asunder
(the people of Makkah requested
Muhammad to show a miracle, so he
showed them the splitting of the moon).

[2.] Yet, when they (disbelievers) see a sign,
they turn away and say
'This is continuous magic.'

[Abdul Hye, 2006 (former NASA engineer)]

There are several short hadith purporting to explain the context of this verse of which the following is typical:

The people of Mecca asked Allah's Messenger to show them a miracle. So he showed them the moon split in two halves between which they saw the Hira mountain.[24]

38. The first permission to fight

Surah 22 (*al-Hajj/The Pilgrimage*): 39

The believers against whom war is waged are given permission to fight in response, for they have been wronged.

Surely, God has full power to help them to victory [40.] Those who have been driven from their homeland against all right, for no other reason than that they say 'Our Lord is God'.

Were it not for God's repelling some people by means of others, monasteries and churches and synagogues and mosques, where God is regularly worshipped and His Name is much mentioned, would surely have been pulled down (with the result that God is no longer worshipped and the earth becomes uninhabitable).

God most certainly helps whoever helps His cause.

Surely, God is All-Strong, All-Glorious with irresistible might.

[*Unal, 2006 (Turkish, Gulen Movement)*]

After more than ten years of preaching in Mecca, Mohammed was invited by some converts from Yathrib (Medina) to leave Mecca and live with them in Yathrib. For two consecutive years, during the main annual pagan pilgrimage to Mecca, this group gathered to meet Mohammed at a place outside Mecca called Aqaba and on the second occasion they swore to protect Mohammed if he returned with them to Yathrib. After this assurance of protection had been given, Mohammed announced a revelation from Jabril that he had been given permission to fight the Meccans. The announcement of the permission to fight is described by Ibn Ishaq as follows:

> The apostle had not been given permission to fight or allowed to shed blood before the second Aqaba. He had simply been ordered to call men to God and to endure insult and forgive the ignorant. The Quraysh had persecuted his followers seducing some from their religion and exiling others from the country. They had to choose whether to give up their religion, be maltreated at home or flee some to Abyssinia, others to Medina.
>
> When the Quraysh became insolent towards God and rejected His gracious purpose, accused His prophet of lying and ill-treated and exiled those who served him and proclaimed His unity, believed in His prophet and held fast to His religion, He gave permission to His apostle to fight and to protect himself against those who wronged them and treated them badly.
>
> The first verse which was sent down on this subject was... {**22.39**}.

In {**22.39**} the permission to fight is justified by retaliation ('*because they have been wronged*') and supported by the observation that violence is sometimes necessary to protect places of worship. This verse is sometimes cited as evidence that Muslims are required to protect all places of worship, although this interpretation goes far beyond the actual text. Moreover, in {**22.41**} the terms of the permission to fight are not expressed as a general right of all people to defend themselves, but rather is a specific permission granted only to those who '*perform the prayer, give the alms, enjoin right and forbid wrong*' (i.e. followers of Mohammed).

Over the following ten years, several other justifications for jihad would be given (see **Part VIII Unbelievers** below).

39. 'Fitna is worse than slaying'
Surah 2 (al Baqarah/The Cow): 191

190. And fight in the way of God against those who fight against you but do not transgress.

Truly, God loves not the transgressors.

191. And slay them wheresoever you come across them and expel them whence they have expelled you, for strife [*fitna*] is worse than slaying.

But do not fight them near the Sacred Mosque until they fight with you there. But if they fight you then slay them. Such is the recompense of the disbelievers.

192. But if they desist, then truly God is Forgiving, Merciful.

193. And fight them until there is no strife [*fitna*] and all is for God. But if they desist then there is no enmity save against the wrongdoers.

[The Study Quran, see ⟨1.⟩]

Shortly after the grant of the first permission to fight, ⟨38.⟩, Mohammed announced a second revelation setting out the terms of the fighting. '*Fitna*', as used in {**Surah 2: 191**, **193**} above, means '*strife*' or '*a trial*' and in this context is understood to refer to resistance to God's will as revealed in the Qur'an.

The phrase '*Fitna is worse than slaying*' is also used in {**2.217**}, see ⟨**40. The raid at Naklah**⟩ following.

40. The raid at Naklah

Surah 2 (*al Baqarah/The Cow*): 217

They ask you about the sacred month, about fighting therein.

Say 'Fighting therein is great (sin), but averting (people) from the way of Allah and disbelief in Him, and (preventing access to) al-Masjid al-Haram and the expulsion of its people therefrom, are greater (evil) in the sight of Allah.

And fitnah is greater than killing.'

And they will continue to fight you until they turn you back from your religion if they are able.

And whoever of you reverts from his religion (to disbelief) and dies while he is a disbeliever: for those, their deeds have become worthless in this world and the Hereafter, and those are the companions of the Fire, they will abide therein eternally.

[*Sahih International, 2010 (three female US converts)*]

Six months after Mohammed's migration from Mecca to Yathrib/Medina his followers conducted their first successful raid on a Meccan caravan, killing one of the four men accompanying it, capturing two others and seizing the goods being transported, which are said to have consisted of raisins and leather.

Several earlier planned raids on Meccan caravans had been aborted, possibly as a result of the Meccans having been alerted by informants in Medina, since on this occasion Mohammed had sent the raiding party out from Yathrib with sealed instructions that they only opened and read after they had travelled for a day. These instructions instructed them to change their direction and to travel south, to conduct their ambush close to Mecca.

By the time that the raid had taken place a traditional Arab month of truce had begun and it is said that when the raiders returned, their community was concerned at this breach of this customary law. These worries were allayed when Mohammed announced the above revelation from God that the duty to attack those who resisted him as God's prophet should take precedence over observing such conventions.

41. The Battle of Badr

Surah 8 (*al-Anfal/The Spoils of War*): 12

Remember thy Lord inspired the angels (with the message) 'I am with you, give firmness to the Believers.

I will instil terror into the hearts of the Unbelievers: smite ye above their necks and smite all their finger-tips off them.'

13. This because they contended against Allah and His Messenger. If any contend against Allah and His Messenger, Allah is strict in punishment.

14. Thus (will it be said) 'Taste ye then of the (punishment): for those who resist Allah, is the penalty of the Fire.'

[*Yusuf Ali/Saudi approved revision, 1985*]

Two months after the raid at Naklah, ⟨**40.**⟩, Mohammed is said to have personally led a raiding party to plunder a much larger Meccan caravan travelling south along the Red Sea coast. The caravan leader was Abu Sufyan, whose daughter, Umm Habiba was a follower of Mohammed and may, according to some accounts, have already been Mohammed's wife (see **D. Mohammed's wives** below). Abu Sufyan was alert to possible attacks and sent out spies who found traces of Mohammed's scouts. When he learned of Mohammed's proximity, Abu Sufyan sent a messenger to Mecca to summon help and altered his caravan's route. Shortly afterwards a hastily assembled Meccan relief force arrived in the area, having missed Abu Sufyan's caravan which returned to Mecca safely by a different route, but finding and engaging with Mohammed's raiding party at the Battle of Badr.

{**54.45-47**} reputedly records the words of Mohammed to his fighters on the morning of the battle:

> 45. The whole shall be routed and they will turn their backs.
>
> 46. Nay! The Hour is their tryst and the Hour is more calamitous and more bitter.
>
> 47. Truly, the guilty are astray and mad.

As it turned out, the confrontation did indeed result in a surprise victory for Mohammed and the deaths of eighty Meccans including some of their most prominent leaders.

The battle is reviewed in the Qur'an in {**Surah 8: 1-17** and **39-48**}. Badr itself is named in {**3.123**} when the survivors of a larger but less disciplined fighting force are urged to reflect how '*God certainly helped you at Badr when you were lowly*'.

After the battle, and the killing of many prominent Meccans in it, Abu Sufyan became the new leader of the Meccan community. A year later he spared Mohammed's life after the Battle of Uhud (**44.**) and he would eventually convert to Islam and surrender Mecca to Mohammed, becoming one of Mohammed's generals. In 661, according to traditional Islamic history, Abu Sufyan's son Muawiyah became the leader of the Muslim community, founding the Umayyad dynasty that presided over the Islamic world for the following ninety years.

42. Treatment of the captives of Badr

Surah 8 (*al-Anfal/The Spoils of War*): 67

> **It is not fit for a Prophet that he should take prisoners of war until he has thoroughly subdued the land.**
>
> **Do you, O followers of Muhammad, desire the temporal goods of this world, while Allah desires for you the hereafter?**
>
> **Allah is Mighty, Wise.**

[*Muhammad Farook-i-Azam Malik, 1997*]

Pickthall and Arberry both translate the opening of {8.67} as: '*It is not for any prophet to have captives until he hath made slaughter in the land*'; Ali Qarai as '*A prophet may not take captives until he has thoroughly decimated (the enemy) in the land*'.

This verse reputedly concerns Meccan prisoners (Ibn Ishaq suggests there were forty-three) that Mohammed had taken at the Battle of Badr. Mohammed is said to have asked his companions what should be done with them, whereupon Abu Bakr advised that they should be released and Umar that they should be killed. In the event Mohammed is reported to have ransomed all his prisoners except for two, whom he ordered to be executed for having mocked him during the time when he had been preaching in Mecca.

A short time later, Umar is said to have found Mohammed weeping. Mohammed informed him that God had revealed this verse to him and that his weeping was due to the belated realisation that God had intended him to kill more of the captives rather than ransom them.

43. Changing the Qibla

Surah 2 (*al Baqarah/The Cow*): 144

We have seen you turning your face
towards the heaven. We shall surely turn
you to a direction that shall satisfy you.

So turn your face towards the Sacred
Mosque (built by Abraham):
wherever you are, turn your faces to it.

Those to whom the Book was given know
this to be the truth from their Lord.

Allah is not inattentive of what they do.

145. But even if you brought those to whom
the Book had been given every proof, they
would not accept your direction, nor would
you accept theirs; nor would any of them
accept the direction of the other.

If after all the knowledge you have been
given you yield to their desires, then you will
surely be among the harm-doers.

[*Qaribullah, see* ⟨12.⟩]

In {**2.155**} and {**2.177**} the Qur'an implies there is no significance to
the direction (*qibla*) in which one faces whilst at prayer:

To God belong the East and West.

Wheresoever you turn, there is the Face of God.

God is All-encompassing, Knowing.

In {**2.144-145**}, by contrast, the physical direction in which one prays is becomes a divine instruction, presented as being an indicator of the orthodoxy of one's faith.

Based upon 1 Kings 8.48 and Daniel 6.11, synagogues are traditionally orientated and Jews pray in the direction of the site of the Jewish temple in Jerusalem. Islamic tradition has it that after Mohammed first arrived in Yathrib/Medina, he required his followers also to face towards Jerusalem when they prayed. Later, it is said, Mohammed announced {**2.144**}, changing the qibla towards the Ka'aba, then a pagan shrine in his birth town of Mecca, (concerning which a supposed biblical heritage would later be claimed, see ⟨**19. Abraham**⟩ above). The *Majid al-Qiblatayn* (the *Mosque of the Qiblas*) in Medina is said to be the place where the change was first announced, causing the congregation to abruptly re-orientate themselves towards Mecca midway through their salat. Subsequently, the mihrab (a niche indicating the direction of the Ka'aba) has become an important element in mosque design.

There is no account of the original Jerusalem qibla having been instructed by God, and it is generally understood by Muslims to have been Mohammed's own preference in order to demonstrate that his revelations were a continuation of the biblical prophecies, and possibly in the hope of encouraging Jewish converts. {**2.144**}'s *'We will turn thee towards a qibla well pleasing to thee'* may suggest that this alignment with Judaism was unpopular with Mohammed's followers whom, it seems, still saw the pagan shrine at Mecca as the focus of their spiritual worldview.

However, it should be kept in mind that neither Mecca not Jerusalem are mentioned in this verse. In *Quranic Geography* (2011) Dan Gibson created controversy when he produced research combining archaeology and GPS readings, indicating that all of the known earliest mosques had in fact originally faced neither Jerusalem nor Mecca, but towards Petra in Jordan.[25]

44. The Battle of Uhud

Surah 3 (*al-Imran/The House of Imran*): 152

Indeed, Allah fulfilled His promise to you when you initially swept them away by His Will, then your courage weakened and you disputed about the command and disobeyed, after Allah had brought victory within your reach.

Some of you were after worldly gain while others desired a heavenly reward.

He denied you victory over them as a test, yet He has pardoned you.

And Allah is Gracious to the believers.

153. (Remember) when you were running far away (in panic), not looking at anyone, while the Messenger was calling to you from behind!

So Allah rewarded your disobedience with distress upon distress.

Now, do not grieve over the victory you were denied or the injury you suffered.

And Allah is All-Aware of what you do.

[Khattab, 2016, (Al Azhar/Canadian Council of Imams)]

After their defeat at the Battle of Badr, the Meccans, now under the leadership of Abu Sufyan, see **⟨41. *The Battle of Badr*⟩** above, marshalled a much larger and better prepared force than the one that they had been able to send at short notice to Badr, with the intention of avenging their losses and crushing Mohammed's growing threat to their trade routes.

The battle is described in some detail by Ibn Ishaq. Mohammed is said to have led his fighters out of Yathrib and to have arranged most of them at the foot of Mount Uhud, with fifty archers deployed on a nearby hill. The battle started well for Mohammed, with the Meccans apparently deterred from using their cavalry by the presence of archers. However, as the battle seemed to be won, the archers left their positions to plunder the Meccan camp, and without their covering fire, the Meccan cavalry was finally able to charge, which it did, scattering the main Muslim force. Mohammed himself was injured by a slingshot to the face, and for a time it was thought by both sides that he had been killed. Thereafter Abu Sufyan called off his attack. Later, when Mohammed had been found alive and helped to a ravine on Mount Uhud he held a shouted conversation with Abu Sufyan, who thereafter permitted him to escape.

The battle is believed to be referred to in **Surah 3** at verses {**121-126**}, which are said to have been announced by Mohammed prior to the battle, and {**140-141, 146-148, 152-158** and **165-168**}. These both console the believers on their defeat:

3.140:

If a wound afflicts you, a like wound has already afflicted that people. And such days in turn we hand out to mankind. And this is so that God may know those who believe and take witnesses from among you and God loves not the wrongdoers,

and seek to explain it as a consequence of their disobedience and greed:

3.152:

And certainly God was true to His promise to you when you were eradicating them by His leave, until the moment you lost heart and quarrelled with one another about the matter and disobeyed after he had shown you that which you loved.

45. *'There is no compulsion in religion'*

Surah 2 (*al-Baqarah/The Cow*): 256

There shall be no compulsion in religion: true guidance has become distinct from error.

But whoever refuses to be led by Satan and believes in God has grasped the strong handhold that will never break.

God is all Hearing and all Knowing.

[*Wahihuddin Khan, 1997
(Indian, onetime follower of Maududi – see ⟨5.⟩)*]

Shortly after the defeat of Uhud, Mohammed announced a revelation that the Banu Nadir, a Jewish clan at Yathrib/Medina had plotted to kill him, and he besieged their compound until they agreed to leave the oasis. Ibn Ishaq recounts that some of Mohammed's Medinan converts had sent their children to the Banu Nadir to raise before their conversion to Islam. On the Banu Nadir's expulsion these converts had asked Mohammed for their children to be returned to them. It is within this context that Mohammed is said to have announced {**2.256**}, that whilst the truth of his revelation of God's words was clear, if the children wished to leave Yathrib with their foster-families they were free to do so.

This verse is often presented as a definitive statement of religious tolerance, although the circumstances of the narration are less than entirely peaceable, and the precise words *'There is* (or *'shall be'*) *no compulsion in religion'* is presented as a statement of fact and do not extend to laying down any general rule as to how Muslims should treat those who are *'led by Satan'* and thus fail to grasp the *'strong handhold'*.

46. The Battle of the Trench

Surah 33 (*al-Ahzab/The Parties*): 10

When they (the disbelievers) invaded you from above (the eastern side of the valley) and from below (the western side of the valley), and when (your) eyes were distracted (with terror), and (your) hearts rose up to your throats (with horror), and you began to think various uncertainties about Allah (in a state of fear and hope).

[*Tahrir Ul-Qadri, see* (**15.**)]

The third and final major military confrontation between Mohammed and the Meccans is said by Muslim histories to have occurred after further attacks by Mohammed on Meccan caravans and Mohammed was increasingly subduing the Bedouin tribes who controlled the land these caravans travelled through.

The Meccans raised their largest force yet, including mercenaries from Africa, and for a second time marched upon Yathrib/Medina. This time, Mohammed kept his fighters within the settlement, which he fortified with a ditch across the only access route suitable for a cavalry charge. The Meccans appear to have been taken by surprise by this tactic and did not attempt to cross the ditch in force. They besieged Mohammed for a month, but suffering from adverse weather, without any plan to breach Mohammed's defences, the Meccans eventually abandoned their siege, without any serious fighting having taken place.

The stand-off is described throughout {**33.9-25**}.

47. Massacre and enslavement of the Banu Qurayza

Surah 33 (*al-Ahzab/The Parties*): 26

He has brought those of the People of the Book (the Jews) who had backed them, down from their fortresses, and cast awe into their hearts, so as to make you kill some of them and take others as captives [27.] and He let you inherit their land and their homes and their wealth, and a land you have not trodden (so far).

And Allah is Powerful to do any thing.

[Usmani, 2007, former Pakistan Supreme Court justice]

Ibn Ishaq reports that immediately following the Meccan retreat from Battle of the Trench, **(46.)** above, Mohammed turned his triumphant army against the last remaining Jewish tribe in Yathrib/Medina. The Banu Qurayza are said to have received messages from the Meccans during the siege urging them to attack Mohammed's forces from the rear in order to distract them and thereby enable the Meccans to storm across the trench. These negotiations had ultimately broken down in mutual distrust.

As a condition of the Banu Qurayza's surrender and to appease those Medinan tribes that had traditionally been allied to it, a member of one such tribe, Sa'd ibn Muadh, was appointed by Mohammed to adjudicate on the allegation of treachery. Sa'd delivered a verdict *'that the men should be killed, the property divided and the women and children taken as captives'.*[26] This sentence was promptly carried out by Mohammed's men, with Ibn Ishaq estimating the number of men killed as between six and nine hundred.[27] This episode provides the only occasion in which Mohammed is reported to have taken a life by his own hand.[28]

The women and children of the Banu Qurayza were enslaved, with Mohammed taking one widow of the massacre, Rayhana, as his own concubine, after she refused his proposal to marry her, saying that to be his slave would be *'easier for her and for him'*.

Some of the captives were later said to have been exchanged for horses and weapons, further increasing Mohammed's military strength.

48. The Treaty of Hudaybiyyah/ The promise of spoils at Kaybar

Surah 48 (*al-Fath/The Victory*): 18

Allah was definitely well pleased with the believers when they, as they sat under the tree, pledged their allegiance to you.

He knew what was in their heart, so He bestowed a comforting calm upon them.

As a reward, He arranged for them a victory in the near future.

19. They will acquire an abundance of booty. Allah is the Mighty, the Wisest.

[Munshey, 2000]

With the horses and weapons purchased with the spoils of the Banu Qurayza and with the Meccans humbled by their failure to capture Medina and proven inability to defend their trade routes, Mohammed led over a thousand followers to Mecca, ostensibly to make a pilgrimage. A Meccan force came out and intercepted him at Hudaybiyyah where the two parties agreed a ten-year truce. For the duration of this truce, Mohammed was promised by the Meccans non-aggression in return for a guarantee that their caravans would be safe from attack.

In **Surah 48 '*The Victory*'**, this treaty is presented as a triumph, guaranteeing '*a victory in the near future*' and '*an abundance of booty*'.

Following the treaty's assurance of Meccan neutrality, Mohammed led his fighters to attack and capture wealthy Jewish settlements at Kaybar, Fadak and Wadi al Qura. At Kaybar, Mohammed is said to have tortured the tribe's leader, Kinana, with fire in order to discover where the tribe's gold was hidden, before killing him, and taking his widow, Safiyya, as his wife (see **D. Mohammed's wives**, below).

Mohammed permitted the Jews of Kaybar to remain on the land subject to a condition that they pay him half their crop as tribute thereafter. This is regarded as the first instance of the acceptance of jizyah, see ⟨53.⟩ below.

Verse {**48.15-16**} suggests that after the Treaty of Hudaybiyyah, some Bedouins who had held back from marching upon Mecca had sought permission to join Mohammed's force to attack Kaybar, no doubt in the hope of partake of its spoils. {**48.16**} refuses them this opportunity, although they are offered future opportunities to earn '*a beautiful reward*' if they agree to fight '*a people of great might*' (probably a reference to a planned raid on an outpost of the Byzantine Empire).

49. The Conquest of Mecca

Surah 17 (*al-Isra/The Night Journey*): 81

And say 'Has come the truth and perished the falsehood. Indeed, the falsehood is (bound) to perish.'

82 And We reveal from the Qur'an that it (is) a healing and a mercy for the believers, but naught it increases the wrongdoers except (in) loss.

[Corpus Coranicumin, an ongoing research project by collaborating international scholars under the auspices of the Berlin-Brandenburg Academy of Sciences and Humanities]

Just two years into the ten-year long agreed truce with Mecca, and with the community that Mohammed led enriched by the proceeds of Kaybar and attracting large numbers of new adherents, Mohammed cited a skirmish between a tribe allied to him and a tribe allied to the Meccans as grounds to declare that the Treaty of Huddaybiyah had been breached and was void.

He marched a force, said by Ibn Ishaq to have numbered ten thousand, upon Mecca. The Meccans caught by surprise and now facing a far stronger foe, sent Abu Sufyan, ⟨41.⟩ ⟨44.⟩, to attempt to negotiate a renewal of the treaty, but when Mohammed refused this, Abu Sufyan agreed to submit to Islam and surrendered Mecca to Mohammed.

Verses {17.81-2}, above, are said to have been announced by Mohammed as he smashed the pagan idols in the Ka'aba.

50. The Battle of Hunayn

Surah 9 (*al-Tawbah/Repentance*): 25

Surely Allah has succoured you before on
many a battlefield, and (you have
yourselves witnessed His succour to you)
on the day of Hunayn when your numbers
made you proud, but they did you no good,
and the earth, for all its vastness,
constrained you.

[*Maududi, see* ⟨5.⟩]

Immediately after the conquest of Mecca, Mohammed organised his fighters, now joined by many Meccan recruits, to march upon the Meccan's traditional enemies to the south, the Banu Hawazin. According to Ibn Ishaq, the Hawazin placed their women and children at the far end of a narrow valley with a line of men at the front of them in order to trick Mohammed into thinking that he was marching towards their main force, then ambushed Mohammed's army from both flanks as it moved down the valley.

{9.25} is said to refer to the foremost Muslim fighters' initial attempt to flee the Hawazin attack but inability to retreat due to the size of the force behind them and the narrowness of the valley. Unable to go back, they were forced to turn again and fight the Banu Hawazin, eventually routing them in what would be the largest battle said to have been fought by Mohammed's fighters in his lifetime.

After the battle Mohammed captured the Hawazin women and children and initially divided them amongst his fighters as spoils of war (see ⟨67.⟩ below) before agreeing to release them in return for the submission of the Hawazin leadership to him.

It was during this allocation of captives that {**4.24**} is reported to have been announced, see ⟨*67. Intercourse with 'those one's right hand possesses'*⟩.

51. The Battle of Tabouk

Surah 9 (*al-Tawbah/Repentance*): 93

God's judgment comes down on those with might,

Who despite their riches, refuse to fight,

Coming to you, for exemption they plead,

Woe unto them, they are weaklings indeed!

A long life they wanted, and with women to stay,

But their lives were destroyed, they were chased away.

Their hearts we have tightly sealed,

The good tidings remain from them concealed,

And revelation with its light

Is forever hidden from their sight.

[Dr Sayfal al-Din Taha, 2005
(poetic interpretation of the Qur'an, believed unpublished)]

In the year following his conquest of Mecca, Mohammed led an army several hundred miles north of Medina to the neck of the Arabian Peninsula in order to attack the town of Tabouk on the frontier of the Byzantine Empire. The verses announced before this expedition repeatedly chide his followers for their lack of enthusiasm for jihad. Further exhortations to sally forth and denunciations of those who failed to, are found elsewhere in {Surah 9: 38-47 and 81-84}.

52. *'The Sword Verse'*

Surah 9 (*al-Tawbah/Repentance*): 5

But when these months, prohibited (for fighting), are over, slay the idolaters wheresoever you find them, and take them captive or besiege them, and lie in wait for them at every likely place.

But if they repent and fulfil their devotional obligations and pay the zakat, then let them go their way, for God is Forgiving and Kind.

[Ahmed Ali, 1984 (Pakistani author/diplomat)]

{**9.5**} are generally considered to be among the last verses of the Qur'an to have been announced, revealed at a time when, according to the traditional Islamic narrative, Mohammed's rule was unchallenged throughout Western Arabia. The verse announces a final solution for those Meccan *'mushrikun'* – those who commit the sin of shirk, the association of things with God, generally translated as pagans, polytheists of idolaters, see ⟨86.⟩ below. These had surrendered to Mohammed two years earlier, but continued to resist conversion to Islam and practice their pagan rituals around the Ka'aba. These recalcitrant unbelievers would now be permitted two months of truce, on the expiry of which they must have professed their acceptance of Mohammed's message and agreed to pay the tax required of believers ⟨57. **Zakat**⟩ or they must be put to the sword.

After announcing the verse in Medina, Mohammed is said to have sent his cousin Ali as a special emissary to Mecca and reveal it to the Meccan pagans during the Muslims' annual pilgrimage.

53. Jizya

Surah 9 (*al-Tawbah/Repentance*): 29

28. O believers, the idolaters are indeed
unclean, so let them not come near the Holy
Mosque after this year of theirs.

If you fear poverty, God shall surely enrich you
of His bounty, if He will; God is All-knowing;
All-wise.

**29. Fight those who believe not in God and
the Last Day and do not forbid what God
and His Messenger have forbidden -
such men as practise not the religion of
truth, being of those who have been given
the Book - until they pay the tribute out of
hand and have been humbled.**

[*Arberry, see* ⟨**16.**⟩]

Whilst under {**9.5**} the Qur'an instructs that '*mushrikun*' must be
slain, see ⟨**52.**⟩ above, '*those who were given the Book*', ⟨**17.**⟩, may be
permitted to live under Islamic rule if they pay '*jizya*', usually
translated as '*tribute*'. The verse is said to have been announced to
provide a means of compensating Meccans who '*feared poverty*'
following the loss of trade with pagan pilgrims, after the
announcement of {**9.5**}: obviously at the expense of unbelievers.

The reference to the payer having been '*humbled*' (alternatively
'*subdued*', '*brought low*', '*humiliated*') indicates that the jizya is
money paid by a non-Muslim to the Islamic state to demonstrate
submission to Islam, rather than a form of taxation for the common
good. Such submitting People of the Book later came to be called
'*dhimmis*' (literally '*protected*') in Islamic societies.

D. Mohammed's wives

Mohammed reputedly married his first wife, the wealthy widow and his employer, Khadija, when he was twenty-five and she was forty. Mohammed was monogamous to Khadija during her lifetime, and they are said to have had six children: two sons, both of whom died in infancy, and four daughters. Without a surviving biological son, they had also adopted a slave, Zayd ibn Harith.

Khadija died in 619. In the twelve years or so following her death, Mohammed is said to have married at least ten more times, accumulating, by the time of his death, nine concurrent wives, which far exceeded the limit of four fixed in {**4.3**}, see ⟨**54.**⟩ and ⟨**60.**⟩ below.

The traditional list of Mohammed's wives following Khadija is:

❖ **Sawda bint Zam'a** (the widow of a follower),

❖ **Aisha** the young child of his friend Abu Bakr,
   see ⟨**59. *Eligibility for marriage*⟩** and ⟨**69. *Making unsupported allegations of sexual impropriety*⟩** below,

❖ **Hafsa bint Umar**, the daughter of Umar, Mohammed's close companion,

❖ **Zaynab bint Khuzayma**, the widow of a Muslim fighter who died at the Battle of Badr, ⟨**41.**⟩, who died shortly following her marriage to Mohammed,

❖ **Umm Salama Hind bint Abi Umayya**, the widow of a Muslim fighter who died at the Battle of Uhud, ⟨**44.**⟩,

- ❖ **Zaynab bint Jahsh**, whom Mohammed's adopted son Zayd divorced in order to permit Mohammed to marry, see ⟨*64.*⟩ below,

- ❖ **Juwayriyyah**, widow of a Bedouin tribal leader killed in a raid led by Mohammed, whose marriage to Mohammed led to the liberation of her enslaved kinsfolk,

- ❖ **Safiyyah bint Huyayy**, the widow of Kinana who was tortured and killed by Mohammed following the Battle of Kaybar, see ⟨*48.*⟩ above,

- ❖ **Umm Habiba Ramla bint Abu Sufyan,** the daughter of Abu Sufyan, who became the Meccan leader following the Battle of Badr, see ⟨*41.*⟩ above; also ⟨*49. The Conquest of Mecca*⟩, and

- ❖ **Maymunah bint al-Harith**.

In addition to these wives, Mohammed is also said to have kept at least two concubines:

- ❖ **Rayhana**, an enslaved widow of the Banu Qurayza, see ⟨*47.*⟩ above, and

- ❖ **Maryam**, a gift of the king of Egypt, see ⟨*68. Intercourse with 'those one's right hand possesses'*⟩ below.

54. Mohammed's wives

Surah 33 (*al-Ahzab/The Parties*): 50

O Prophet! We have made lawful to thee thy wives to whom thou hast paid their dowers,

And those whom thy right hand possesses out of the prisoners of war whom Allah has assigned to thee,

And daughters of thy paternal uncles and aunts, and daughters of thy maternal uncles and aunts, who migrated (from Makka) with thee,

And any believing woman who dedicates her soul to the Prophet if the Prophet wishes to wed her; this only for thee, and not for the Believers (at large).

We know what We have appointed for them as to their wives and the captives whom their right hands possess, in order that there should be no difficulty for thee.

And Allah is Oft-Forgiving, Most Merciful.

[Yusuf Ali, 1938 (British-Indian; until recently this was the most widely read English translation)]

This verse legitimises marriage either by the voluntary entry of the two partners into a marriage contract ('*nikah*') or by a man taking as his 'wife' a female captive that had been allocated to him as his share of the spoils of war, as Mohammed had done with Juwayriyyah and Safiyyah.

This verse, and also {**33.37**}, is traditionally treated as having been announced in relation to Mohammed's marriage to Zeynab bint Jahsh. This marriage had scandalised Mohammed's followers for two reasons.

One issue was that Mohammed's marriage to Zeynab made her his fifth wife, which breached the rule in {**4.3**} that a man may have only four wives at one time, see **(60.)** below.

The second, more serious, problem was that Zeynab had previously been married to Mohammed's adopted son, who had divorced her in order to enable her marriage to Mohammed to take place, which made the marriage seem incestuous.

This latter issue was dealt with by a revelation that an adopted son did not become a part of a person's family, see **(65. *Adoption*)** below, but both impediments are also overcome with the more generally worded permission granted to Mohammed to marry: '*any believing woman who dedicates her soul to the Prophet if the Prophet wishes to wed her; this only for thee, and not for the Believers (at large)*'.

It is this verse that reputedly caused Aisha to remark to Mohammed that '*Your lord hastens to fulfil your desires.*'[29]

55. Rules for Mohammed's wives

Surah 33 (*al-Ahzab/The Parties*): 33

32. O wives of the Prophet, you are not like anyone among women.

If you fear Allah, then do not be soft in speech (to men), lest he in whose heart is disease should covet, but speak with appropriate speech.

33. And abide in your houses and do not display yourselves as (was) the display of the former times of ignorance. And establish prayer and give zakah and obey Allah and His Messenger.

Allah intends only to remove from you the impurity (of sin), O people of the (Prophet's) household, and to purify you with (extensive) purification.

[*Sahih International, see* **(40.)**]

In verses {**33.28-33**} the Qur'an prescribes special rules for the wives of Mohammed who are declared to be '*not like other women*'. These rules include doubling the sentence for a '*flagrant indecency*', {**33.30**}, see **(69. Fornication and Adultery)** below. Presumably this was announced in relation to {**24.2**} rather than {**4.15**}, since it is impossible to double a capital sentence.

In {**33.53**} Mohammed's wives are told to '*abide in their homes*' and '*flaunt not their charms*', and the same verse prohibits any man from marrying any of Mohammed's wives after his death, see **(56. Rules for visiting Mohammed's house)** below.

In addition, {**66.1-2**} permits Mohammed to break his oath to his wives and the following verses include a warning from God to the wives of Mohammed that he may replace them with more devoutly obedient wives should they incline against him.

66.3-5

3. When the Prophet confided a certain matter to one of his wives, but she divulged it, and God showed it to him, he made known part of it and held back part of it.

When he informed her of it, she said 'Who informed thee of this?'

He replied, 'The Knower, the Aware informed me.'

4. If you both repent unto God for your hearts did certainly incline, and if you aid one another against him, then truly God, He is his Protector, as are Gabriel and the righteous among the believers, and the angels support him withal.

5. It may be that if he divorces you, his Lord would give him wives in your stead who are better than you, submitting, believing, devoutly obedient, penitent, worshipping, and given to wayfaring — previously married, and virgins.

These verses clearly refer to some incident in which one of Mohammed's wives was believed to have broken his confidence. Two narration accounts of these verses exist, both involving jealousy on the part of Hafsa towards Maryam. In one account, Hafsa complained to her co-wives that Mohammed had had intercourse with Maryam on Hafsa's allocated day and even in Hafsa's apartment. In the other, possibly created to provide a more reputable explanation, Hafsa and Aisha had conspired to try to make Mohammed believe that Maryam's honey made his breath smell, in order to sow discord between the two of them.[30]

56. Rules for visiting Mohammed's house

Surah 33 (*al-Ahzab/The Parties*): 53

O Ye who believe! enter not the houses of
the Prophet, except when leave is given you,
for a meal and at a time that ye will have to
wait for its preparation; but when ye are
invited, then enter, and when ye have eaten,
then disperse, without lingering to enter
into familiar discourse.

Verily that incommodeth the Prophet, and
he is shy of asking you to depart, but Allah
is not shy of the truth.

And when ye ask of them aught, ask it of
them from behind a curtain. That shall be
purer for your hearts and for their hearts.

And it is not lawful for you that ye should
cause annoyance to the apostle of Allah,

Nor that ye should ever marry his wives
after him; verily that in the sight of Allah
shall be an enormity.

[Daryabadi (1892-1977), British Indian]

This verse sets out rules for visitors to Mohammed's house. In an
assertion that seems at odds with all other indications of his
character, Mohammed is described to be '*shy*' to ask his guests to
depart his house immediately after a meal, but is spared doing so
by God who is '*not shy*' to set down this rule on Mohammed's
behalf.

VI

Sharia

E. The Five Pillars of Islam

The Qur'an is traditionally said to set down five positive obligations upon Muslims individually (*fard al-ayn*), popularly called, following a hadith,[31] the '*five pillars of Islam*'.

These are:

- ❖ professing the Shahada declaration of faith, see ⟨12.⟩ above,

- ❖ performing Salat, five daily prayers, see ⟨33.⟩ above,

- ❖ fasting during the month of Ramadan, see ⟨78.⟩ below,

- ❖ Giving zakat (compulsory alms), see ⟨57.⟩ following, and

- ❖ making the hajj pilgrimage if one is able, see ⟨19.⟩ above.

57. Zakat

Surah 9 (*al-Tawbah/Repentance*): 60

Zakat is but a vehicle of prayers. It is due only to:

> the poor who are destitute of means of livelihood, and
>
> the needy who are in temporary distress due to sickness, disability or the like,
>
> those who are engaged as collectors and administrators thereof, and
>
> those who have just reconciled themselves with their own hearts and with Allah,
>
> those in bondage who are eager to buy their freedom,
>
> those in debt who are genuinely unable to pay what is owed to others,
>
> the support of the cause of Allah,
>
> and the wayfarer -who does not have the means for transportation and has to travel on foot.

This is an obligation incumbent on Muslims and dutiful to Allah.

[Al-Muntakhab, see ⟨2.⟩]

Paying zakat (literally *'that which purifies'*, commonly translated as *'alms'* or *'regular charity'*) is one of the 'five pillars' of Islamic piety (see *E. The Five Pillars of Islam*, above).

A general duty to give alms is instructed in several verses of the Qur'an, see *(83.)* below. However, there is a separate requirement to make a payment of zakat that, unlike the general duty, is expressed in specific, formal terms. To emphasise its nature as a regulated and enforced payment, {**9.60**} makes provision for the *'collectors and administrators'* of zakat to take a share of the money they collect; in several places, including {**17.26**}, the recipient's share is described as his *'due'* (*'haqahu'*); and in {**6.141**} a time is prescribed for its donation: *'Eat of (various listed) fruit when they grow and pay the due thereof on the day of its harvest'*.

In {**4.77**}, {**9.5**}, see *(52.)* above, {**9.11**} and {**22.41**}, see *(38.)* above, paying zakat is presented as an essential condition to being recognised as a believer. In {**41.7**} failure to make the payment is equated with disbelief.

The quantum of zakat is not prescribed in the Qur'an but it is traditionally levied at one fortieth of a Muslim's capital assets, paid annually on the first day of each Islamic new year.

58. Usury

Surah 2 (*al Baqarah/The Cow*): 275

Those who swallow usury will not rise,
except as someone driven mad by Satan's
touch.

That is because they say 'Commerce is like
usury.'

But God has permitted commerce and has
forbidden usury.

Whoever, on receiving advice from his
Lord, refrains, may keep his past earnings,
and his case rests with God.

But whoever resumes — these are the
dwellers of the Fire, wherein they will
abide forever.

[*Itani, see* ⟨25.⟩]

Usury ('*riba'*) is the charging of interest on loans. It is
condemned in the Qur'an at {**2.275**} above and also at {**3.130**,
4.161} and {**30.39**}.

These verses were no doubt aimed at promoting generosity and
preventing exploitation at a time before modern capitalist
economies could have been anticipated. Consequently, many
Muslims treat the verses as prohibiting only the charging of
excessive interest on a loan, although this inevitably introduces
an element of subjectivity into the prohibition. Others interpret
the rule strictly, and 'halal' accounts are now offered by many
banks.

59. Eligibility for Marriage
Surah 65 (*al-Talaq/Divorce*): 4

And as for those who gave up hope of
menstruation among your women,
if you were in doubt, their waiting period is
three months and for those who have not
yet menstruated.

As for those who are imbued with
pregnancy, their term is that they bring
forth their burden.

And whoever is Godfearing of God,

He will make his affair with ease for him.

[*Laleh Bakhtiar, 2007 (Iranian-US, author and psychiatrist)*]

In both {**2.221**} and {**5.4**} the Qur'an states that a believing man may
marry a woman '*of the Book*' ⟨**17.**⟩, whether she is free or a slave.
From the fact that both of these verses refer to marrying women, it
has generally been held in Islam to be impermissible for a believing
woman to marry an unbeliever, although the issue is not explicitly
addressed.

{**4.22-23**} sets out a number of family relationships within which
individuals are '*mahram*' – unavailable for marriage – to one
another.

In {**2.228-9**} a declaration by a man that he has divorced his wife is
not to be treated as final until such time as the divorced wife has
subsequently menstruated three times, see (**62. Divorce**) below. In
{**65.4**} the Qur'an sets a substitute period of three (lunar) months
for two classes of women who do not menstruate: namely, '*those*

who no longer await menstruation' and *'those who are yet to menstruate'.* By so doing, the Qur'an necessarily endorses marriage to premenarchal girls.

Before having left Mecca, Mohammed, then aged fifty-two, is reported to have married Aisha, the six-year-old daughter of his friend Abu Bakr. In hadiths, attributed to Aisha, she states that she was playing with dolls shortly before the marriage ceremony took place and that she began living with Mohammed three years later, in Medina, at the age of nine.[32]

These ages of Aisha at her marriage contract and at the consummation of it are cited in the major classical hadith collections, and by Ibn Hishem as a note to his preserved copy of Ibn Ishaq's biography of Mohammed, although not by Ibn Ishaq himself.

Since the early twentieth century, some Muslims have challenged the above accounts of the age of Aisha, constructing timelines from the account of her reported age difference from her elder sister Asma and Mohammed's daughter Fatima, and their reported ages, in an attempt to demonstrate that Aisha must have been older than six at the time of her marriage. The novel interpretation is also sometimes now suggested that the second category of women mentioned in {**65.4**} refers only to adult women who do not menstruate because they suffer from amenorrhea. However, this is a rare medical condition and it is unusual for the Qur'an, when prescribing rules, to make specific provision even for much more commonplace illnesses and disabilities.

60. Polygamy

Surah 4 (*al-Nisa*/*Women*): 3

**If you are afraid of not behaving justly
towards orphans, then marry other
permissible women, two, three or four.**

**But if you are afraid of not treating them
equally, then only one, or those you own as
slaves.**

**That makes it more likely that you will not
be unfair.**

[*Abdalhaqq and Aisha Bewley, 1999 (husband and wife)*]

The phrase '*two or three or four*' (which also appears in {**35.1**}, see
⟨**4.**⟩ above) although capable of being read as an idiom meaning
'*several*', is traditionally read literally as prescribing four as the
maximum number of wives that a man may have at one time. One
hadith tells of a man with ten wives who converted to Islam and
who was instructed by Mohammed to choose four of his wives to
retain and to renounce the other six.[33]

The connection between the care of orphans and polygamy is
cryptic. It may be a comparison between the duty to act virtuously
to orphans and a similar duty with regard to wives.

This verse also confirms a man's right to 'marry' his slaves, and
here so doing is presented as a possible solution to a man's fear that
he would be unable to treat multiple free wives equitably.

See also ⟨**54. Mohammed's wives**⟩ above.

61. Beating one's wife for disobedience

Surah 4 (*al-Nisa/Women*): 34

Men are the protectors and maintainers of
women, because Allah has made one of
them to excel the other, and because they
spend (to support them) from their means.

Therefore, the righteous women are
devoutly obedient (to Allah and to their
husbands), and guard in the husband's
absence what Allah orders them to guard
(e.g. their chastity, their husband's property,
etc).

As to those women on whose part you see
ill-conduct, admonish them (first),
(next), refuse to share their beds,
(and last) beat them (lightly, if it is useful),
but if they return to obedience, seek not
against them means (of annoyance).

Allah is Ever Most High, Most Great.

[*Hilali & Khan, see* ⟨**14.**⟩]

It is clearly the Qur'an author's hope that parties to a marriage will
live together in amity:

30.21

And among his signs is that he created mates for
you from among yourselves, that you might find
rest in them, and He established affection and
mercy between you.

Truly in that are signs for a people who reflect.

In the Qur'an, maintaining domestic peace is founded upon a man's right of authority over his wife and a wife's duty of obedience to her husband. This is justified upon the natural order as fixed by God: *'because Allah has made one of them to excel the other'*; see also {**2.228**}: *'And men have a degree over (women)'*. A second justification offered is the wife's presumed financial dependence on her husband, (although this presumption seems somewhat incongruous, given Mohammed's own early financial dependence upon his first wife, the successful businesswoman and his former employer, Khadija.)

Where his wife fails to demonstrate the requisite level of obedience to her husband, {**4.34**} provides the husband three sanctions: admonishment, *'sending to beds apart'* (deriving from *'h-j-r'*– the same word as is used for Mohammed's migration from Mecca to Yathrib, (*38.*): effectively *'sulking'*[34]) and physical chastisement.

{**4.34**} is said to have been revealed to cause Mohammed to repeal an order that he had made moments earlier that a man brought before him should be punished for having beaten his wife, so severely that *'her skin was as green as her cloak'*. Many translations qualify *'strike'* or *'beat'* with some mitigating words such as *'(lightly)'*, based upon *hadith* in which Mohammed is said to have instructed that a man should not beat his wife with a weapon, or on her face, or in the same way that he would beat a slave or camel, immediately before lying with her.[35]

62. Divorce

Surah 2 (*al-Baqarah/The Cow*): 229

A divorce is only permitted two times:
After that the parties should either stay
together on just terms, or separate with
kindness.

It is not lawful for you (men) to take back
any of your gifts (from your wives) except
when both parties fear that would be
unable to keep the limits set forth by Allah.

If you (judges) do fear that they would be
unable to keep the limits set forth by Allah,
then there is no blame on either of them if
she gives something for her freedom.

These are the limits set by Allah, so do not
break them.

If any (person) does step beyond the limits
set forth by Allah, such persons wrong
(themselves as well as others).

[*Syed Vickar Ahamed, 1999 (Al Azhar, a simplified translation aimed at younger readers)*]

{2.228} prescribes that when a man declares his wife to be divorced the divorce is not final and may still be revoked by him at any time until the woman has had, since the declaration of divorce, three menstrual cycles (subject to {65.4}, see ⟨59.⟩ above).

{2.229} qualifies {2.228} so that if a man declares his wife divorced three times (the so-called '*triple talaq*') then he may no longer revoke the divorce. This rule was reportedly (*per* Ibn Kathir, author of the most frequently cited Qur'an commentary) introduced some time after {2.228} in order to stop one particular Muslim man repeatedly divorcing his wife and thereafter revoking the divorce, thereby preventing her from remarrying.

There is a consensus within Islam that Qur'an contains no equivalent right for a wife to declare her husband divorced. However, a wife may negotiate the terms of a divorce (*kuhl*) with her husband, which normally involves her paying him for her release from the marriage (*'there is no blame on either of them if she gives something for her freedom'*). It is also generally held that that should her husband fail to agree reasonable divorce terms, a wife may petition a Sharia court/tribunal to impose such terms - although to obtain an imposed khul divorce requires that the applicant show serious fault on the part of her husband such as abandonment, failure to meet the obligation of maintenance, or excessive violence (see ⟨*61.*⟩).

63. Weaning

Surah 2 (*al-Baqarah/The Cow*): 233

Mothers should breastfeed their children
two full years, provided they want to
complete the nursing. The family head must
support women and clothe them properly.
Yet no person is charged with more than he
can cope with.

No mother should be made to suffer
because of her child, nor family head
because of his child. An heir has the same
(duties) in that respect.

If they both prefer to wean (the child) when
they have agreed terms and consulted
together, it should not be held against them;
so if you want to find a wet-nurse for your
children, it should not be held against you,
provided you hand over whatever you may
have given in all decency.

Heed God and know that God is Observant
of anything you do.

[Irving/Ta'lim Ali, 1985 (Canadian convert)]

In the event that a man divorces his wife whilst she has a young
child by him, the man is obliged to support them both for up to two
years. Sharia jurists differ over whether this verse implies that a
man has the right to reclaim his child from their mother at the end
of the weaning period or later when the child reaches puberty.

64. Adoption

Surah 33 (al-Ahzab/The Parties): 5

4. God does not put two hearts within a man's breast.

He does not turn the wives you reject and liken to your mothers' backs into your real mothers, nor does He make your adopted sons into real sons.

These are only words from your mouths, while God speaks the truth and guides people to the right path.

5. Name your adopted sons after their real fathers: this is more equitable in God's eyes – if you do not know who their fathers are (they are your) 'brothers-in-religion' and proteges. You will not be blamed if you make a mistake, only for what your hearts deliberately intend.

God is most Forgiving and Merciful.

[Abdel-Haleem, see ⟨13.⟩]

These verses were said to have been announced in the context of the marriage of Mohammed to Zaynab bint Jahsh. Zeynab had been married to Zaid ibn Harith, whom Mohammed had previously adopted as his son, see ⟨54.⟩ above. Zaid is said to have divorced his wife to enable Mohammed to marry her, after Mohammed had inadvertently seen her undressed, and had declared that the sight had *'caused his heart to turn'*.

The consequences of the announcement of this verse are that, under Sharia law, a child that is looked after by an adoptive family, retains their biological father's name and, for the purposes of administering estates according to the ordained shares set out in {**Surah 4: 11-12** and **176**}, an adopted child stands to inherit from their biological relatives, but not from their adoptive family.

An associated verse relating to Mohammed's renunciation of Zaid as his son, {**33.40**}, reads:

> Muhammad is not the father of any man amongst you. Rather he is the Messenger of God and the seal of the prophets.
>
> And God is the knower of all things.

In his book *Muhammad Is Not the Father of Any of Your Men, The Making of the Last Prophet*, David S. Powers argues that this renunciation was critical for the final editors of the Qur'an, to depict Mohammed - the *'seal of the prophets'* - as having died without a male heir, in order to prevent his son in law, Ali, from establishing a dynasty for Mohammed's grandchildren.

65. Inheritance

Surah 4 (*al-Nisa/Women*): 11

Allah prescribes (the following) law
(of inheritance) for your children.

For male is the equal of the portion of two
females;

but if they be all females (two or) more than
two, for them is two thirds of what he (the
deceased) has left; and if there be only one,
for her is the half,

and for his parents, for each one of the two
is a sixth of what he has left, if he (the
deceased) has a child; but if he has no child
and his parents only be his heirs, then for
the mother is one third (and the rest two
thirds is for the father); but if there be (in
addition to his parents) his brothers (and
sisters) then there is one sixth for the
mother after (the payment of) any bequest
he may have bequeathed or (still more
important) of any debt (bequests made by
the testator and his debts shall however be
satisfied first).

Your fathers and your children, you do not
know which of them deserve better to
benefit from you.

(This) fixing (of portions) is from Allah.

Surely, Allah is All-Knowing, All-Wise.

[*Omar and Omar, see* (27.)]

{2.180} encourages Muslims to write a will, and {2.240} requires them to bequeath at least a year's subsistence to their widows.

{4.11-12}, later supplemented by {4.176} (see also {4.7-9}), prescribe a mathematical formula for dividing an estate between relatives. A hadith[36] resolves the discrepancy between the two methods of distributing an estate – according to a will or by divinely ordained shares - recording that Mohammed permitted up to one third of an estate only to be bequeathed, the balance to be distributed according to the divinely ordained shares.

Probably the most conspicuous aspect of the ordained shares formula is the gender inequality. Under {Surah 4: 11-12 and 176}, a daughter receives half as much as a son, a wife half as much as her husband would have done, and where a deceased person leaves no children, a sister half as much as her brother. This unequal distribution is traditionally justified on the basis that a woman is usually provided for by their biological family or their husband (see {4.34} 'men are the protectors and maintainers of women', (61.) above) throughout their life, and consequently a women's financial needs are less than those of men. In this way inheritance and marriage laws operate together to determine the dependent role of women in a Sharia-governed society.

The complexity in applying the ordained shares formula outlined in the above verse, especially within the elaborate family structures that result from the practices of polygamy and consanguineous marriages, is often credited as having provided the incentive for the Muslim world's development of probably its greatest contribution to secular learning: algebra.

66. Slavery

Surah 16 (*al-Nahl/The Bee*): 71

Allah has made some of you excel in
sustenance over the others; those who are so
favored, do not give away their sustenance
to their slaves so as to make them their
equals.

How can you think that Allah will allow
other deities to be His equals?

Would they refuse to acknowledge the
favors of Allah?

[*Farook Malik, see* ⟨42.⟩]

Several verses in the Qur'an regulate the possession of slaves, and
six verses of the Qur'an provide for the manumission of slaves:

as act of piety {**90.13**},

out of charity {**9.60**},

as a penance to be performed for accidentally causing the
death of a Muslim {**4.92**} or for breaking the terms of an
oath {**5.89**} and {**58.3-4**}, or

in return for payment {**24.33**}.

However, no verse disapproves of slavery, and indeed the sanction
of releasing a slave would seem to require the continued
availability of slaves to free. In {**16.71**} slavery is hailed as one of
God's means of blessing the slave owner, and freeing slaves for the
purpose of making the slave and master equal is discouraged.

See also ⟨67. *Intercourse with 'those one's right hand possesses'*⟩.

67. Intercourse with
'those one's right hand possesses'
Surah 4 (*al-Nisa/Women*): 24

And all married women (are forbidden unto you), save such as your right hands possess (captives of war); it is a decree of Allah for you

But lawful for you are all beyond these.

So seek them with your wealth in honest marriage and not lust.

[*Hamid Aziz, 1981*]

According to the traditional chronological order of Quranic revelations, by the time of the announcement of {4.24} three Qur'an verses {23.1-9, 70.19-35} and {33.50} (see ⟨54.⟩ above) had already stated that a believing man would not be guilty of adultery in relation to his own marriage(s) by having sexual intercourse with a female *'whom his right hand possesses.'* After the Battle of Hunayn, see ⟨50.⟩ above, which took place two weeks following Mohammed's conquest of Mecca, some Meccans who had only recently joined Mohammed's army were uncertain whether they would be committing adultery in relation to their captives' marriages, by having intercourse with prisoners whom they knew were married. Mohammed revealed this fourth verse on the subject, clarifying that a man was permitted to have sex with his captive, even if that person had been married when captured.

Mohammed is said to have kept at least two slave concubines: Rayhana, see ⟨47.⟩ above, and Maryam, who had been sent, with her sister, as a gift from the king of Egypt and who bore Mohammed his only child after the death of Khadija.

F. Punitive sanctions in the Qur'an

The Qur'an prescribes set punishments for three types of misconduct (known as *'hudud'* offences):

- ❖ fornication/adultery, see ⟨**68.**⟩ below,
- ❖ making an unsupported allegation of sexual impropriety, see ⟨**69.**⟩ below, and
- ❖ theft, see ⟨**71.**⟩ below.

In addition:

- ❖ although no sentence is specifically fixed for engaging in homosexual acts, such conduct might reasonably be treated as constituting, at the very least, a species of fornication/adultery, see ⟨**70.**⟩ below, and
- ❖ based upon the hadith, some schools of Sharia law also include blasphemy, apostasy, drinking alcohol and gambling ⟨**72.**⟩ as *hudud* offences.

For the more loosely defined offences of *'waging war upon God'* and *'spreading corruption on the earth'* the Muslim ruler may choose from four sanctions: execution, crucifixion, amputation from opposite sides and exile, see ⟨**73.-74.**⟩ below.

All other wrongs are dealt with by a system of qisas: the imposing, at the discretion of the victim or their family, of an injury upon the perpetrator equivalent to the harm suffered by the victim, see ⟨**75.**⟩ below.

68. Fornication and adultery

Surah 4 (*al-Nisa/Women*): 15

**As for those of your women who may
commit whoredom, call against them four
witnesses from among them if they testify,
confine you them to their houses till death
complete their turn of life, or Allah appoint
for them some other way.**

[Daryabadi, see ⟨56.⟩*]*

In {**4.15**} a sentence of confinement until death is fixed for those
who commit a sin (*'fahishah'*) – generally translated as *'indecency'* or
'fornication' - whilst in {**24.2**} a sentence of one hundred lashes is
fixed for the crime of *zina* – generally interpreted as adultery.
Neither term is defined in the Qur'an, and the two punishments
seem inconsistent, since the graver of the two offences is prescribed
the lighter of the penalties. To complicate matters, numerous
hadith[37] describe Mohammed ordering adulterers to be stoned to
death – a sentence that appears nowhere in the Qur'an itself.

The process by which these sources have been reconciled by Sharia
jurists is convoluted. Some rely upon a hadith that Mohammed
adopted the stoning sanction straight from God's revelation in the
Torah.[38] A different hadith describes how a *'stoning verse'* was
announced by Mohammed, but that the paper upon which it had
been written was eaten by a goat as Mohammed lay dying.[39] Most
jurists concluded that, given the sheer number of hadith reporting
Mohammed ordering stoning, this must be the appropriate
sentence for adulterers, with whipping for fornicators.

The number of lashes for indecency is halved for slaves {**4.25**} - but
doubled for the wives of Mohammed {**33.30**}, see ⟨55.⟩ above.

69. Making an unsupported allegation of sexual impropriety

24 (*al-Nur/Light*): 4

And as for those who accuse chaste women (of adultery), and then are unable to produce four witnesses (in support of their accusation), flog them with eighty stripes and ever after refuse to accept from them any testimony - since it is they, they that are truly depraved!

[5] Excepting (from this interdict) only those who afterwards repent and made amends.

For, behold, God is much forgiving, a dispenser of grace.

[*Asad, see* ⟨**17.**⟩]

A narration account[40] relates this rare rule of evidence to an accusation of sexual impropriety made against Aisha (see **D. Mohammed's wives**, above). Aisha, so the account goes, had been accompanying Mohammed on an expedition when she left their camp to look for a lost necklace and became stranded. Eventually she was rescued by a male member of the expedition, but when the two of them rejoined the main group, three people spread speculation that Aisha and the man had committed adultery. This same incident is also said to have prompted the announcement of {**24.11-24**}.

{**24.4**} seems to set an almost impossible bar for prosecutions for infidelity where there is no admission or pregnancy. Whereas this may work to avoid, for many, the harsh sanctions for fornication, where the rule is applied for the protection of men as well as women, it has an unfortunate, and probably unintended, consequence. Should a woman accuse a man of having raped her, without having four witnesses to corroborate her account, she may find herself in the legal position of having admitted that intercourse with the man had taken place whilst having her accusation against her attacker dismissed. This leaves the victim of such a crime in jeopardy of being whipped for fornication or stoned for adultery, depending upon her marital status, whilst the true guilty party is protected from any sanction, however compelling the circumstantial evidence of his guilt may be.

70. Homosexuality

Surah 26 (*al-Shu'ara/The Poets*): 166

165. What! Among all the creatures,
you commit the immoral acts with men?
[166] **And leave the wives your Lord has
created for you?**

**In fact, you are people who exceed the
limits.**

[*Ahmed Raza Khan, 1910, subsequently translated from Urdu to
English by Faridul Hacque (Khan is a key figure in the Barelvi
movement, the largest Pakistani Sufi tradition)*]

The Qur'an contains four clear condemnations of homosexuality:
at {7.80-84, 26.160-172, 27.54-58, 29.28}, all within the context of a
retelling of the story of Lot. In Genesis, chapter 19, Lot had
sheltered two angels in his house, which was then besieged by a
crowd of men from the nearby city of Sodom intent on committing
homosexual rape upon them. Later, Lot was warned to leave the
place to avoid God's anger and he fled as Sodom and neighbouring
Gomorrah were destroyed by fire and brimstone for their
wickedness. In the Qur'an, unlike Genesis, it is unambiguously the
practice of homosexuality itself (rather than the element of assault)
that attracts God's wrath.

In addition, some also consider that {4.16} - '*And if two of those
among you are guilty thereof,* (i.e. of indecency) *punish them both, but
if they repent and make amends, then let them be*' - may have been
intended to relate to homosexuality. The argument goes, that the
phrase '*two of those amongst you*' may be inferred to relate to two
men, since the Qur'an would appear to have been primarily
addressed to a male congregation.

Although no sentence is fixed for homosexuality in the Qur'an, most Muslim jurists consider homosexual acts to be a type of fornication (to be dealt with by a hundred lashes), or adultery (stoning to death) if either of the parties was married. A hadith relates Mohammed considering an accusation of homosexuality and ordering his followers *'to kill the one who does it, and the one to whom it is done'*.[41] Another hadith attributes to Ali, Mohammed's son in law and the fourth caliph, the practice of killing homosexuals by throwing them from tall buildings, choosing for his condemned prisoners, the minaret of a mosque.

71. Theft

Surah 5 (*al-Ma'idah/The Table Spread*): 38

Cut off the hands of a male or female thief
as a punishment for their deed and a lesson
for them from God.

God is Majestic and All-wise

[*Sarwar, see* ⟨2.⟩]

Hadith state that Mohammed instructed that this rule should be applied strictly to anybody who stole an item worth as little as the value of an egg or a rope.[42]

Schools of Sharia law differ as to how to deal with repeat offenders. The jurist Abu Hanifa ruled that no more than one hand and one foot should be amputated, even where an offender continued to steal, further offending no doubt becoming more difficult to commit after the loss of two limbs; and subsequent offences were to be dealt with by incarceration only. He reasoned that a person would be unable to comply with ritual cleansing if their second hand were to be taken. The Sha'afi and Hanbali schools, however, apply no such limit, considering that {**5.38**} requires that all four limbs may be taken for four consecutive offences.

72. Consuming alcohol and gambling

Surah 5 (*al-Ma'idah/The Table Spread*): 90

O you who believe! Intoxicants, gambling, idolatry and divination are abominations of Satan's doing.

Avoid them, so that you may prosper.

91. Satan wants to provoke strife and hatred among you through intoxicants and gambling, and to prevent you from the remembrance of God, and from prayer.

Will you not desist?

[*Itani, see* ⟨25.⟩]

The Qur'an's approach to alcohol appears to have become progressively censorious.

In {**16.66-67**} wine was presented as a blessing from God:

We give you to drink… from the fruits of the date palm and the vine from which you derive strong drink and a goodly provision.

{**4.43**} warns against attending prayers whilst drunk.

In {**2.219**} drinking alcohol and gambling are treated as twinned vices and are warned against together.

Finally, in {**5.90-91**} above, both the consumption alcohol and gambling are condemned outright as '*abominations of Satan's doing*', see ⟨*7. Iblis and al-Shaitan*⟩.

Hadith record Mohammed ordering drunkards to be flogged.[43]

73-74 'Working corruption on the earth'
Surah 5 (*al-Ma'idah/The Table Spread*): 32-33

> 32. On account of (his deed), We decreed to the Children of Israel that if anyone kills a person - unless in retribution for murder or spreading corruption in the land - it is as if he kills all mankind, while if any saves a life it is as if he saves the lives of all mankind.
>
> Our messengers came to them with clear signs, but many of them continued to commit excesses in the land.
>
> 33. Those who wage war against God and His Messenger and strive to spread corruption in the land should be punished by death, crucifixion, the amputation of an alternate hand and foot, or banishment from the land: a disgrace for them in this world, and then a terrible punishment in the Hereafter.

[*Abdel-Haleem, see* ⟨12.⟩]

{**5.32**} is one of the most oft quoted - and misquoted – passages of the Qur'an, often cited without the following verse that completes its meaning.

Several hadith record the circumstances in which two verses were announced as relating to some Bedouins who had killed a Muslim camel herder and stolen his livestock. They were pursued and brought before Mohammed, who *'cut off their hands and feet and gouged their eyes. They were left in this state in Medina until they died.'*[44]

In {**5.32**} the Quranic author, speaking as always in God's voice, purports to recall instructions He had given previously to the Israelites. In fact, however, the phrase that follows come not from God's words in the Torah but from a second or third century Jewish commentary upon the Torah, the *Mishna Sanhedrin* (reflecting upon Cane's murder of Abel in chapter 4 of Genesis). In this, the commentator muses that to kill a person who is still capable of having children, is not only to kill that person but to kill the infinite number of potential descendants whose existence he might otherwise have brought about (an early articulation of what today would be called the 'butterfly effect'):

> *Therefore man was created as a single being in the world in order to teach that anyone who causes a single life to perish is considered to have caused an entire world to perish and anyone who preserves a single life is considered to have preserved an entire world.*

{**5.33**} presents a new instruction on dealing with the offences of '*waging war against God and His Messenger*' and '*endeavouring to work corruption upon the earth*'. This permits a judge to choose from four punishments - although it will be noted that in the episode that gave rise to this announcement, Mohammed is reported to have inflicted sentence that exceeded even the four {**5.33**} options.

The term '*hirabah*', that is here translated as '*endeavouring to work corruption*' (as it is by Arberry and Pickthall), alternatively rendered '*making mischief*' (Yusuf Ali), appears in several other verses of the Qur'an as a generic term for human propensity to wickedness contrasted with virtue (for example in {**2.11**, **2.220**} and {**3.63**}). Based upon the hadiths referred to above, and possibly to restrict the power of the early caliphs, Sharia lawyers have interpreted '*hirabah*' in {**5.33**} as a specific type of offence, analogous with banditry. Even so, the verse is clearly intended to give Muslim rulers a wide discretion in defining, and imposing draconian punishments for, deviation from the Sharia.

75. Qisas

Surah 5 (*al-Ma'idah/The Table Spread*): 45

**And We ordained for them in (the Torah):
A life for a life, and an eye for an eye,
and a nose for a nose, and an ear for an ear,
and a tooth for a tooth, and a (similar)
retribution for wounds,**

**But he who shall forgo it out of charity will
atone thereby for some of his past sins.**

**And they who do not judge in accordance
with what God has revealed, they are the
evildoers!**

[*Asad, see* ⟨**17.**⟩]

As {**5.45**} acknowledges, the system of imposing upon an offender an injury equivalent to the injury that they have caused (*lex talionis*) appears in the Torah,[45] although the earliest known use of the famous phrase '*An eye for an eye and a tooth for a tooth*' is in fact much older even than that, forming part of the Babylonian Code of Hammurabi (c. 1750 BC).

By contrast, Jesus had taught (Matthew 5.38-39):

> *You have heard the commandment 'An eye for an eye,
> a tooth for a tooth'. But what I say to you is: offer no
> resistance to injury. When a person offers you their
> right cheek, turn and offer him the other.*

The Islamic system of *qisas*, provides that a victim or their next of kin, is offered a formal election whether to inflict the proportionate injury or to take compensation in lieu. The practical effect of this middle way is that either the Sharia state engages in the mutilation of offenders, or that an offender with means may avoid the painful punishment that a poorer person may incur, through the payment of *diyah*, sometimes referred to as '*blood money*'.

The regime is further expounded upon, in relation to causing a death, in {**2.178**}:

> O you who believe! Retribution is prescribed for you in the matter of the slain. Freeman for freeman, slave for slave female for female.
>
> But for one who receives any pardon from his brother, let it be observed honourably, and let the restitution be made to him with goodness.
>
> That is an alleviation from your Lord and a mercy.
>
> Whoever transgresses after that shall have a painful punishment.

On the face of the text, {**2.178**} would appear to instruct that as a punishment for a killing, a life should be taken of equal 'value' to the life of the victim: whether freeman, slave or woman. However, the verse is invariably interpreted to mean merely that a perpetrator should not face death in qisas for taking a life that is deemed to be less valuable, according to the freeman-slave-female hierarchy, than their own.

{**17.33**} states that, wherever a person is slain unjustly, '*We have appointed authority*' to claim either the inflicting of qisas or the payment of diyah, on behalf of the deceased person '*unto his heir*'.

This has the practical consequence that an heir will have to balance the public interest and/or personal satisfaction of requiring retribution, against the killer of their relative, against their own material self-interest or the potential benefit to other family members of accepting compensation. It also lays open to the way for a wealthy offender to 'buy their way out of trouble' in a way that would not be possible for a poorer one.

The strict wording of {17.33} also raises a specific conundrum where a person stands simultaneously in the position of both killer and heir. In a hadith, Mohammed is said to have ruled that '*the son is to suffer retaliation for* [killing] *his father but the father is not to suffer retaliation for* [killing] *his son*'[46] and this was the position taken, at least in relation to capital punishment, by all the major early jurists.

See also ⟨29. *'Al Khidr'*⟩ above. For an additional punishment for homicide, see ⟨76. *Killing believers and covenantors*⟩ below.

76. Killing believers and covenantors

Surah 4 (*al-Nisa/Women*): 92

It is not for a believer to kill another believer, except that it is by error.

Whosoever kills a believer in error, let him free a believing slave, and ransom is to be handed to his family, unless they forgo being charitable.

If he belonged to a people who are your enemies and is a believer then, the setting free of a believing slave.

If he belonged to a people in which there is between you and them a treaty, then a ransom is to be handed to his family and the setting free of a believing slave.

But, if he does not find (the means) let him fast two consecutive months in repentance to Allah.

And Allah is the Knower, the Wise.

[*Qaribullah, see* ⟨12.⟩]

By prescribing a separate sanction for each of the following:

1. killing a believer,
2. killing a believer with whom the killer is in a state of enmity, and
3. killing an unbeliever with whom the killer had a covenant

{4.92}, by necessary implication, anticipates that a believer who kills a non-believer with whom they did not have a specific covenant, should face no punishment.

This interpretation is consistent with numerous expressions of intense hostility to unbelievers set out in **Part VIII** below. In particular it accords with the closely following verse {**4.94**}:

> O you who believe! When you go forth in the way of God, be discerning and say not unto him who offers you peace 'You are not a believer' seeking the ephemeralities of the life of the world, for with God are abundant spoils.
>
> Thus were you yourselves beforehand but God has been gracious to you. Therefore be discerning.
>
> Truly God is aware of whatsoever you do.

Hadith[47] state that this verse was revealed after one or more incidents in which Muslims had robbed and killed victims who had offered the Islamic greeting of peace. Muslims are here urged to '*be discerning*' and not to lightly reject professions of belief as false, and risk killing fellow believers, through desire for '*the ephemeralities of this world*' i.e. loot. It seems to be implicit in the instruction to take due care not to kill a fellow believer, that the act of killing a non-believer should be regarded as unobjectionable.

77. Dietary rules

Surah 5 (*al-Ma'idah/The Table Spread*): 3

Forbidden to you (for food) are carrion, blood, the flesh of swine, what has been (slaughtered) in the name of any other than that of Allah, and the beast strangled, beaten to death, killed by a fall, the gored to death by a horn, and that which same wild beast has begun to eat, (all are unlawful), except what you slaughter (in accordance with the prescribed law). And (also forbidden is to you) what has been slaughtered before idols, or that you divide by the arrows: (all) that is ungodliness.

Today those who disbelieve have despaired of your religion, so do not dread them but dread Me.

Today have I perfected your religion for you, and completed My favour on you, and I have chosen for you Islam as a religion.

But, whoever is helplessly forced by hunger, without inclining to sin, (can enjoy of the forbidden food), then verily Allah is Forgiving, Merciful.

[*Sayyed Abbas Sadr-ameli, see* ⟨7.⟩]

Dietary rules are also set out in {2.172-173, 6.118, 6.142-147} and {16.114-115} (and permission to eat in certain settings in {24.61}). The prohibition on eating animals that have been '*beaten to death*' is the scriptural basis put forward for opposition to stunning animals before slaughter, due, it is claimed, to concern lest an animal die of shock between the stun and its death through exsanguination.

78. Fasting

Surah 2 (*al-Baqarah/The Cow*): 183

It was in the month of Ramadan that the Koran was revealed, a guide for mankind with proofs of guidance and salvation.

Therefore, whoever of you is present in that month let him fast.

[184.] And he who is ill or on a journey shall fast a similar number of days later on.

God desires your well-being, not your discomfort.

He desires you to fast the whole month so that you may magnify God for His guidance and render thanks.

[*Dawood, see* ⟨22.⟩]

The obligation to fast, from dawn to dusk, during the lunar month of Ramadan is one of the '*five pillars of Islam*' (see **E. The Five Pillars of Islam**, above).

79. 'Women are a tilth to you'
Surah 2 (al Baqarah/The Cow): 223

Your wives are as a tilth unto you,
so approach your tilth when or how ye will,
but do some good act for your souls
beforehand, and fear God.

And know that ye are to meet Him (in the
Hereafter) and give (these) good tidings to
those who believe.

[*Yusuf Ali, 1938, see* ⟨**54.**⟩]

A '*tilth*' is an archaic term for land used for crop-growing, sometimes translated as '*a ploughed field*'. '*Go unto your tilth as you will*' is clearly intended to permit men a degree of freedom to engage in sexual activity with their wives – with an implicit suggestion of a right to impregnate them. The metaphor of a woman as a field in which her husband may plant his seed is consistent with the Qur'an writer's understanding of reproductive biology, whereby a human being develops entirely from a man's 'seed' – '*a drop emitted*' (per Yusuf Ali) produced from between the '*loins*' (alternatively '*backbone*') and the ribs {**86.6-7**} in which the mother's role is merely one of providing a womb.

Hadith relate this verse both to a wife's duty to comply whenever her husband desires intercourse, several employing the Arabic idiom '*even if riding a camel,*'[48] and also to the permissibility of different sexual positions - although the precise scope of the sexual positions or activity that are permitted by this verse is unclear and, inevitably, a fertile ground for disagreement.

80. Modest female attire

Surah 33 (*al-Ahzab/The Parties*): 59

O Prophet! Tell your wives, your daughters, and women of the believers that they should draw their outer garments over their person (when in public).

This is easy and proper, so that they may be recognized and not bothered.

Allah is Absolver of imperfections, Merciful.

[*Shabbir Ahmed, 2003 (Pakistani-US)*]

{33.59} is one of two Qur'an verses addressing the attire of women in general, the other being {24.31}.

In addition {33.33} instructs the wives of Mohammed specifically to '*Abide in your homes and flaunt not your charms as they did flaunt them in the prior Age of Ignorance*' (55. *Special rules for Mohammed's wives*) below.

It is noteworthy that none of these verses explicitly requires a woman to conceal their hair or face, in the style that has become iconic for Muslim women and girls. Whether the word '*jilbab*' in {33.59}, that is variously translated as '*outer garments*' (above), '*cloaks*', '*wraps*', '*veils*', '*wrapping garments*', '*overgarments*' or '*chadors*', necessarily implies a head covering, depends upon a question of seventh-century Arabian sartorial usage that is now unanswerable. However, since {24.31} specifies that women should:

> ... draw their kerchief over their breasts, and
> not display their adornment ... (*except to certain*
> *classes of people: husbands, close family, etc*)

> ... (*and not*) stamp their feet such that the
> ornaments that they conceal become known ...

this verse, at least, may be seen as implicitly permitting uncovered heads. The possibility that it directs a believing woman to cover their upper chest, but assumes that their hair, let alone face, is already covered, can surely be dismissed as fanciful.

The 'covering up' instruction in {**24.31**} is linked with chastity and seems aimed at encouraging women to adopt concealing attire for reasons of modesty, but {**33.59**} offers a different reason: '*Thus it is likelier that they will be known and not disturbed*'. This rationale indicates that the Qur'an author anticipates that women who would be '*known*'- presumably identifiable as believers through their enveloping dress rather than recognised individually – would consequently be spared being '*disturbed*' (or in other translations '*harassed*' or '*molested*'). The verse does not spell out how being readily identifiable as a Muslim would protect a woman from being harassed but it is suggested that the only plausible explanation is that the Qur'an author has in mind harassment by believing men, who, it is hoped, would not disturb a member of their own community.

81. The testimony of women

Surah 2 (*al Baqarah/The Cow*): 282

O you who have believed, when you contract a debt for a specified term, write it down. And let a scribe write (it) between you in justice.

Let no scribe refuse to write as Allah has taught him. So let him write and let the one who has the obligation dictate.

And let him fear Allah, his Lord, and not leave anything out of it.

But if the one who has the obligation is of limited understanding or weak or unable to dictate himself, then let his guardian dictate in justice.

And bring to witness two witnesses from among your men. And if there are not two men (available), then a man and two women from those whom you accept as witnesses - so that if one of the women errs, then the other can remind her.

And let not the witnesses refuse when they are called upon.

And do not be (too) weary to write it, whether it is small or large, for its (specified) term.

That is more just in the sight of Allah and stronger as evidence and more likely to prevent doubt between you, except when it is an immediate transaction which you conduct among yourselves. For (then) there is no blame upon you if you do not write it.

And take witnesses when you conclude a
contract. Let no scribe be harmed or any
witness. For if you do so, indeed, it is
(grave) disobedience in you.

And fear Allah.

And Allah teaches you.

And Allah is Knowing of all things.

[Sahih International, see ⟨40.⟩]

{2.282} (which is the longest verse in the Qur'an) directs, amongst
other things, that the record of a debt should ideally be witnessed
by two men, but that, should two men not be available, an
attestation by one man and two women may suffice. The verse
provides a rationale for this gender specificity, namely that women
have a greater tendency to forgetfulness than men.

Although the literal scope of the rule is limited to records of debt,
some schools of Islamic jurisprudence have drawn broader
evidential rules from this verse including the inadmissibility of
women's testimony on most matters and a legal presumption that,
where testimonies conflict, a woman's testimony be afforded half
the weight afforded to that of a man. Such rules remain a feature
of litigation in many Sharia-based legal systems today.

IX
Virtuous behaviour

82. Honesty

Surah 83 (*al-Mutaffifin/The Defrauders*): 1

Woe unto the scrimpers.

2. Those who, when they take by measure from mankind, exact the full, [3] and who, when they measure unto them or weigh for them, diminish.

4. Imagine such men not that they shall be raised up [5] on a Mighty Day,
[6] a Day whereon mankind shall stand before the Lord of the worlds?

[*Daryabadi, see* ⟨55.⟩]

The two practical transactions in which honesty is illustrated in the Qur'an are the giving of full measure and dealing equitably with property held on trust.

Giving false measure is condemned in {83.1-6} above, {17.35} and {55.8-9}. This also appears to have been the principal sin of the people of Midian, who are reproached for it by the prophet Shuaib in three verses ({7.85, 11.84, 26.181-183}, see ⟨26.⟩ above.)

Honouring trusts, is instructed at {4.58, 8.27, 23.8} and {70.32}.

In {4.29} the Qur'an contains a general call for honesty in trade:

O you who believe! Consume not each other's wealth falsely but trade by mutual consent and slay not yourselves.

Truly God is merciful unto you.

83. Generosity

Surah 4 (*al Nisa/Women*): 36

And worship none but God and raise none
to His Divine level.

Show kindness to and help your parents,
the relatives, the orphans, the needy ones,
the neighbors (related or non-related to
you), the stranded traveller and your slaves.

Know that God does not like the arrogant
show-offs who are stingy, reproach people
for being charitable and hoard what God
has blessed them out of His kindness.

[Bijan Moeinian, 2005 (Iranian-US)]

A call to give voluntary alms, is made directly in {2.177, 23.4, 27.3, 30.39} and {31.4} and is referred to indirectly, for example as part of God's covenant with the people of Israel, or instructions from the mouths of Ishmael and the infant Jesus, in several other places: {2.43, 2.83, 5.12, 7.156, 19.31, 19.55} and {21.73}.

Since believers are bound to pay obligatory alms in the form of zakat, ⟨57.⟩, as an essential requirement of being a believer, the duty to give discretionary alms should be seen as a separate, additional but more flexible duty.

The above list of those to whom charity should be given – parents and other relatives, orphans, those in need, travellers and one's slaves – mirrors the list of obligatory zakat recipients in {9.60} and also appears, with slight variations at {Surah 2: 177 and 215} and

{**30.38**} and indirectly, as a recalled past instruction to the Children of Israel at {**2.83**}.

Obligatory zakat is traditionally only distributed amongst Muslims. The above verses, taken in isolation, are broad enough that they might be interpreted in such a way that a Muslim should, in appropriate cases, show generosity, born of compassion, to '*the needy ones, the neighbour who is not of kin...* (and) *the traveller'* without confessional discrimination. However, since Muslims must strive to interpret the Qur'an as a consistent whole, these verses are hardly specific enough to be read as overruling the many verses urging separation from and hostility towards unbelievers. (see **Part VIII** below).

84. Respect for others

Surah 49 (*al-Hunjurat/The Private Apartments*): 12

11. O You who have chosen to be graced with belief! No folk shall make mockery of other folk, for they may be better than they are. Nor shall any women ridicule other women, for they may be better than they are.

And neither shall you defame one another, nor insult one another by nicknames. Bad is the immoral name after attaining faith.

And whoever turns not, such are wrongdoers.

12. O You who have chosen to be graced with belief! Avoid much suspicion and guesswork. For, behold, some of such suspicion and guesswork deplete your communal energy.

And spy not upon one another, nor shall you backbite one another. Would any of you like to eat the flesh of his dead brother?

Nay, you would detest it!

Be mindful of Allah. Verily, Allah is Relenting, Merciful

[*Shabbir Ahmed, 2003 (Pakistani-US)*]

Believers are called to shun slander, insults, gossip and spying on one another. Regarding the latter, {24.27-28} instructs believers not to enter houses without having first sought the occupant's permission and offered a greeting, whilst {2.189} prohibits entering another person's house by the back door. In hadith, Mohammed angrily threatens a follower for peering into his house whilst he was combing his hair.[49] {17.23} prohibits showing disrespect, represented as saying the word '*uff*' to one's parents.

85. 'Repel evil with good'

Surah 41 (*Fussilat/Expounded*): 34

The good deed and the bad deed are not equal!

Repel (the bad) with that which is best...

Then you will see, the person who had enmity towards you will be like as though he was a devoted friend!

[*Hulusi, 2013 (Turkish Sufi)*]

Some verses of the Qur'an encourage patience and forbearance in the face of opposition, such as:

2.109:

Many of the people of the book wish to turn you back into disbelievers after your having believed, out of envy in their souls, even after the truth has become clear to them.

So pardon and forebear, until God comes with his Command.

Truly God is powerful over all things.

and

3.186:

You will surely be tried in your wealth and your souls and you shall hear much hurt from those who were given the Book before you and from those who are idolaters.

But if you are patient and reverent, then that is
indeed a course worthy of resolve.

See also {**5.13**} in relation to apostates: '*Thou wilt not cease to discover their treachery, from all save a few of them. So pardon them and forebear. Truly God loves the virtuous*'.

This sentiment is often presented with the motif of '*repelling evil with good*' {**13.22**, **28.54**} and {**41.34**} above, or '*by that which is better*' {**23.96**}, or to '*pardon and set matters aright*' {**42.40**}. In a similar vein, {**60.7**} reads:

It may be that God will forge affection between
you and those of them with whom you are in
enmity.

God is Powerful, and God is Forgiving,
Merciful.

Other verses recommend the avoidance of arguments with unbelievers but encourage saying '*Peace*' instead {**25.63**} and {**43.89**}.

{**5.48**} instructs believers to '*vie with one another in good deeds*'.

All these verses appear to be directed at the sphere of personal relationships, rather than the application of law. As with generosity (see ⟨*83.*⟩ above) it is implicit in the Qur'an, read as a whole, that the qualities of '*goodness*' and '*evil*' should be determined, by a Muslim, not subjectively but within the context of the whole of the Sharia.

.

VIII

Unbelievers

86. Believers and unbelievers

Surah 49 (*al Hujarat/The Apartments*): 14

The Arabs (often mistranslated as nomads or
Bedouins) said 'We believed'.

Say 'You did not believe but say
"We submitted/became Moslem"
and the faith/belief did not enter in your
hearts/minds.

And if you obey God and His messenger He does
not reduce/diminish you a thing from your deeds,
that truly God (is) Forgiving, Merciful'.

[*Muhamed Ahmed and his daughter Samira, 1994 (Canadian)*]

One of the most prevalent themes of the Qur'an is the division of
humanity into believers and unbelievers, who are praised or
denounced, and promised rewards or threatened with
punishment, in this world and the next, accordingly. Almost one
in six of the verses of the Qur'an addresses or refers to the believers
('*al-mu'minum*'). The non-believers are referred to variously as:

> '*kaffir*': literally '*those who conceal (the truth)*';
>
> '*mushrikun*': literally those who commit shirk, the sin of
> associating something with God, (see **(1.)** above), often
> translated as '*pagans*', '*polytheists*' or '*idolaters*', but
> probably intended, at least in some verses, to include those
> who believe in the divinity of Jesus;
>
> '*hypocrites*';

or specifically identified as Christians, Jews, Sabians and Magi,
who are collectively called People of the Book, see **(17.)** above.

A central theme of Fred M. Donner's *Muhammad and the Believers* is that {**49.14**} demonstrates a distinction between what it is to be a believer and a Muslim.

> *Belief obviously means something different (and better) than 'submission' (islam); and so we cannot simply equate the Believer with the Muslim, though some Muslims may qualify as believers.*
>
> *The Qur'an's frequent appeal to the Believers, then – usually in phrases such as 'O you who believe' – forces us to conclude that Muhammad and his early followers thought of themselves above all as being a community of Believers rather than one of Muslims.*

The foundation of every verse in the Qur'an is the premise that the listener accepts the authenticity of the Qur'an itself as God's final revelation A summary of the doctrines that one must hold to be true in order to be counted as a '*believer*' appears to be given in {**2.285**}, see ⟨**17.**⟩ above.

However, how the phrase '*Each believes in God ... and His messengers. We make no distinction between any of His messengers*' in {**2.285**} should be applied to Jews and Christians who follow previous prophets sent by God but do not accept Mohammed as the '*seal of the prophets*', see ⟨**12.**⟩ above, is unclear and the Qur'an's treatment of Jews and Christians may well vary from one surah to another. As outlined through the remainder of this Part, there are certainly many verses where Christians and Jews are named and shamed as non-believers.

To illustrate of the inconsistency, **Surah 30** begins by reviewing a military defeat suffered by Byzantine Empire (almost certainly its loss of Damascus and Jerusalem to the Sassanian Empire in 614-5):

2. The Byzantines have been defeated [3.] in a land nearby.

Yet after being defeated they will prevail [4.] within a few years – unto God belongs the affair, before and after and on that day the believers shall rejoice [5.] in God's help.

He helps whomever He will and He is the Mighty, the Merciful.

The clear implication here is that Catholic Byzantium[50] was, at the time of the announcement of this verse, regarded as a part of the community of believers. However, by {48.16}, see ⟨*48. Treaty of Hudaybiyyah and the promise of the spoils of Kaybar*⟩ above and and the Battle of Tabouk ⟨51.⟩ the Byzantine Empire had been identified as a legitimate target for jihad, ⟨91.⟩

In 2007, as a response to a controversial lecture addressing Islam (and Byzantium) given by Pope Benedict XVI the previous year, an open letter entitled '*A Common Word Between us and You*' was signed by 138 prominent Islamic scholars, said to represent '*every denomination and school of thought in Islam*' to the world's Christian leaders, to '*declare the common ground*' between Christianity and Islam.

The letter uses the Pickthall (*see* ⟨6.⟩ above) translation of {3.64}, a verse was said to have been revealed when Mohammed was visited by a delegation of Christians from Najran, in Yemen, and discussed the differences between Christianity and Islam with them.

Say 'O People of the Scripture! Come to a
common word between us and you:

that we shall worship none but God, and that
we shall ascribe no partner unto Him, and that
none of us shall take others for lords beside
God.'

And if they turn away, then say
'Bear witness that we are they who have
surrendered (unto Him)'.

However, the word '*sawa*' that Pickthall renders as '*common*'
literally means '*level*', '*sound*' or '*central*', and idiomatically '*the right
way*'[51] rather than a shared '*common ground*'. Moreover, the verse's
explicit linking of its call to a '*common word*' to the rejection of
'*ascribing any partner unto*' God - an obvious call to repudiate the
Christian belief in the divinity of Jesus - suggests that the
ecumenical interpretation put upon {**3.64**} by the Muslim scholars
was probably not one originally intended by the verse's author.

87. Unbelievers are *'the worst of creatures'*

Surah 8 (*al-Anfal/The Spoils of War*): 55

The worst of creatures in God's view are those who disbelieve. They have no faith

56. Those of them with whom you made a treaty, but they violate their agreement every time. They are not righteous.

57. If you confront them in battle, make of them a fearsome example for those who follow them, that they may take heed.

[*Itani, see* ⟨25.⟩]

The condemnation of unbelievers, or *'kafir'*, ⟨86.⟩, as *'the worst of creatures'*, above,(alternatively *'the worst of beasts'* per Arberry, Pickthall, Yusuf Ali; *'the vilest of animals'*, etc) is one of several verses that dehumanise those who do not believe in the Qur'an's message. Others include:

7.179:

We have indeed created for Hell, many among jinn and men: they have hearts with which they understand not ... Such as these are like cattle. Nay, they are even further astray.

and

98.6:

Truly the disbelievers among the People of the Book and the idolaters are in the fire of Hell, abiding therein.

It is they who are the worst of creation.

In {**5.59-60**} the Qur'an addresses the People of the Book, see ⟨**17.**⟩ above, '*most of* (whom) *are iniquitous*', and whom '*God has cursed and upon whom is His Wrath and among whom he has made some to be apes and swine*'.

The reference to God having turned some People of the Book into apes and swine, may be connected to verses {**2.65**} and {**7.166**} in each of which God recalls having cursed Jewish sabbath-breakers by saying '*Be ye apes*'. It is unclear on whether these verses refer to some lost tradition that God once turned some Jews into apes, or if the Qur'an is merely using the animal terms as generic insults, but {**5.60**} seems clearly to be intended to be taken literally. If the Jews are in other verses associated with apes, this may tend to associate the pigs in {**5.60**} with Christians: the porcine transformation possibly due with the acceptability in Christianity of eating swine.

Another dehumanizing image for unbelievers is employed in {**7.175-176**} in relation to '*the one to whom we gave our signs, but he cast them off*', sometimes associated with an Arabian poet and contemporary of Mohammed, Umayyah ibn Abi Salt.

> ...Thus his parable is that of a dog. If you attack him he lolls his tongue and if you leave him alone he lolls his tongue.
>
> That is the likeness of the people who deny Our signs.'

88. 'Al-wala wal bara' (Loyalty and rejection)

Surah 48 (al-Fath/The Victory): 29

> Muhammad is the apostle of God,
> and those who are with him are strong
> against Unbelievers, (but) compassionate
> amongst each other....

[Yusuf Ali, 1938, see ⟨54.⟩]

The Qur'an requires believers to maintain a clear division between themselves and infidels. It instructs believers ten times not to take unbelievers as *auliyah* (usually translated as *'friends'* or, probably more authentically, *'allies'*) in preference to other believers. These are found at:

{**3.28**}, see ⟨*90. Taqiyyah*⟩ below,

{**Surah 4: 88-9**, **139** and **144**},

{**5.51-2**}, with specific reference to Jews and Christians,

{**5.57**}, with specific reference to those who mock the signs of God,

{**5.80**}, {**8.73**},

{**9.23**}, with specific reference to family members,

and {**13.16**}.

It also contains two, similarly worded calls for believers to apply a double standard to others depending upon their faith or lack thereof: {**48.29**} above and {**5.54**}:

O you who believe!

Whosoever among you should renounce his religion, God will bring a people whom He loves and who love him, humble toward to believers, stern toward unbelievers, striving in the way of God (waging jihad) and fearing not the blame of any blamer...

This doctrine of self-segregation is sometimes referred to by the Arabic maxim *'al-wala wal bara'* (*'loyalty and rejection'*).

Through these verses the author no doubt seeks to build the believers in the Qur'an into a distinct and mutually supportive community within the context of a society based upon clan loyalty and an ongoing conflict. Nevertheless, even allowing for the historical setting, these repeated instructions promoting sectarianism are in marked contrast with most other religions' promotion of inclusivity and even-handedness.

89. Kindness to unbelievers not forbidden

Surah 60 (*Mumtahanah/She Who Is Examined*): 8

**Allah does not forbid you from showing
kindness to and from behaving with full
equity towards those (of the non-believers)
as do not fight against you because of (your)
faith, nor drive you out from your
homelands.**

**Allah does indeed love those who act
equitably.**

9. Allah forbids you from getting close in
friendship only with such as fight against
you because of (your) faith, and drive you
out, and aid and abet in driving you out,
from your homelands.

And those (among you) who lean towards
them in friendship — those then are the
wicked ones!

[Muhammad Shafi Deobandi]

A hadith[52] links this verse to a visit to an incident shortly after
Mohammed's migration to Yathrib/Medina in which Asma, a
daughter of Abu Bakr and sister of Mohammed's wife Aisha, ⟨D.
Mohammed's wives⟩, ⟨59.⟩, received a visit from her unbelieving
mother, bringing her gifts of cheese and lizards. Before admitting
her mother, Asma is said to have gone to ask Mohammed if she
was permitted to do so, whereupon she received the above verse
in reply.

90. *Taqiyyah*

Surah 3 (*al Imran/The House of Imran*): 28

Let not the believers take the disbelievers for friends rather than believers.

And whoever does this has no connection with Allah - except that you guard yourselves against them, guarding carefully.

And Allah cautions you against His retribution. And to Allah is the eventual coming.

[*Maulana Mohammed Ali, 2010, (Lahore Ahmadiyya)*]

This verse is sometimes relied upon by critics of Islam as approving the use of deceit as a hostile strategy against unbelievers. This understanding of *taqiyyah*, however, is based less upon the text of this passage, than upon the comments of Ibn Kathir, in the most widely read Qur'an commentary, in relation to it:

('*...except that you guard yourselves against them, guarding carefully*') *meaning 'except those believers who in some areas or times fear for their safety from the disbelievers.' In this case, such believers are allowed to show friendship to the disbelievers outwardly, but never inwardly.*

For instance, al-Bukhari recorded that Abu Ad-Darda [a companion of Mohammed] *said: 'We smile in the face of some people although our hearts curse them.'*

See also {16.106}.

91. Meaning of Jihad

Surah 9 (*al-Tawbah/Repentance*): 19

> Do you regard the providing of water to
> Hajj pilgrims and the maintenance of the
> Holy Mosque as similar (in worth) to
> someone who has faith in Allah and
> (believes in) the Last Day and wages jihad
> in the way of Allah?
>
> They are not equal with Allah, and Allah
> does not guide the wrongdoing lot.

[*Ali Qarai, see* ⟨19.⟩]

The well-known word '*jihad*', in one form or another, appears forty-one times in thirty verses of the Qur'an. The word has a literal meaning of '*to strive*' or '*to struggle*' and on occasion in the Qur'an the word may be translated in this general sense. However, it is most often used, especially in the phrase '*to strive in God's way*', in the more specific and widely understood sense of engaging in holy warfare in the cause of Islam. In addition, there are many other verses that instruct religious-military action using the less ambiguous word '*qital*' (to fight). Some of these go beyond a mere permission or instruction to engage in violence but amount to rallying exhortations:

<u>2.216</u>:

> Fighting has been prescribed for you, though it is
> hateful to you.
>
> But it may be that you hate a thing though it be
> good for you and it may be that you love a thing
> though it be evil for you.
>
> God knows and you knows not.

8.65:

O Prophet! Rouse the believers to fight.

If there be twenty steadfast amongst you, they shall overcome two hundred. And if there by one hundred of you they shall overcome one thousand of those who disbelieve, because they are a people who understand not.

47.35:

Truly those who disbelieve and turn from the way of God, then die while they are disbelievers, God will not forgive them.

35. So do not falter and call for peace while you have the upper hand.

God is with you and will not deprive you of your deeds.

61.4:

Truly God love those who fight in his way in ranks as if they were a solid structure.

See also:

{**8.12**}: *'So strike above their neck and strike their every fingertip'*, see ⟨**41. The Battle of Badr**⟩,

{**9.5**}: *'Capture them and besiege them and lie in wait for them at every place of ambush'*, see ⟨**52. 'The Sword Verse'**⟩, and

{**9.36**}: *'Fight the idolaters all together, just as they fight you all together'*, see ⟨**94. Rules of war**⟩, and

{**9.123**}: *'Fight those believers who are near to you and let them find in you harshness.'*

The nobility of those who wage jihad is celebrated in {**2.218**, **5.54**, **8.74**, **9.41-44**} and {**61.4**} above.

An oft-cited hadith has Mohammed contrasting military jihad with the *'greater jihad'* of *'striving against inner desires'* (*'jihad al-nafs'*, literally *'jihad with oneself'*). However this account is not contained within any of the major collections of hadith and can only traced back as far as the eleventh century, making it a certain late forgery.[53]

On the contrary, {**9.19**}, above, unambiguously lauds combat over non-combat service. The same point is made in {**4.95**}, which states that those believers who *'stay behind'* are not equal with those who *'strive (make jihad) in God's way'*, *'save for those that are disadvantaged'* (i.e. disabled), demonstrating that the phrase *'jihad in God's way'* refers to a physical rather than spiritual struggle.

92. Reasons for jihad

Surah 9 (*al-Tawbah/Repentance*): 26

Then God sent down a sense of tranquillity on His Apostle and the faithful and sent down troops invisible to punish the infidels.

This is the recompense of those who do not believe.

[Ahmed Ali, see ⟨52.⟩]

Some verses of the Qur'an encourage patience and forbearance in the face of opposition (see ⟨*85. 'Repel evil with good'*⟩). However, these are outnumbered, and, if the verses are read in their traditional chronological order, qualified or superseded by verses instructing violence (see ⟨*11. Abrogation*⟩ above).

At least nine reasons are given in the Qur'an for militant jihad:

1. righteous retribution

    {**22.39-41**} '*for they* (the believers) *have been wronged*', see ⟨38.⟩, and

    {**9.12**}; '*if they renege on their oaths after having made their treaty, and vilify your religion, then fight the leaders of disbelief ... that they might desist*';

2. to capture Mecca {**4.74-6**};[54]

3. to remove an obstacle or challenge to the practice of Islam

> {**2.217**}, see ⟨**40.**⟩, and {**9.12**}, see above,
>
> {**4.89**}: '*They wish that you should disbelieve even as they disbelieve, that you may be on a level with them. So take them not as protectors till they migrate in the way of God. But if they turn their backs, then seize them and slay them wherever you find them, save those who seek refuge with a people with whom you have a covenant or those who come to you with hearts reluctant to fight you, or to fight their own people*';

4. as a demonstration of God's power

> {**8.7-8**} '*God desires to verify the truth through his words and to cut off the last remnant of the unbelievers*',
>
> {**8.57**} '*If thou comest upon them (unbelievers) in war, use them to scatter those who will come after them that haply they might be reminded.*'
>
> {**8.67**} see ⟨**42.**⟩, and {**48.18-20**}, see ⟨**48.**⟩;

5. as a test for believers {**47.4**}, see ⟨**93.**⟩ above;

6. to reward Muslims with the spoils of war

> {**3.145**} '*Whosoever desires the reward of this world, We shall give him of it … And we shall reward the thankful*' (relating to the Battle of Uhud, see ⟨**44.**⟩),
>
> {**9.28-9**}, see ⟨**53. Jizya**⟩,
>
> {**33.27**} '*And He bequeathed unto you their land, their homes, their property and a land you have not trodden*' (relating to the Banu Qurayza, see ⟨**47.**⟩),

{**48.18-20**} *'God has promised you abundant spoils that you will capture'* (relating to Kaybar, see **⟨48.⟩**);

7. fighting believers who oppress their fellow believers

> {**49.9**} *'If two parties among the believers fall to fighting, make peace between them. If one of them aggresses against the other, fight those who aggress until they return to God's Command...'*;

8. to expand the territory where the rule of Islam prevails and eliminate disobedience to God's will therein

> {**2.191-3**}, see **⟨39.⟩**, and {**2.217**}, see **⟨40.⟩**: *'Fitna is worse than slaying'*,
>
> {**8.12-7**} *'I shall cast terror into the hearts of those who disbelieve, ...that is because they are in schism with God and His Messenger'*, see **⟨41.⟩**,
>
> {**8.39**} *'And fight them until there is no fitna and religion is wholly for God'*,
>
> {**24.55**} *'God has promised those among you who believe and perform righteous deeds that He will surely make them vice-regents upon the earth'*,
>
> {**48.28**} *'He it is who sent His Messenger with guidance and the religion of truth to make it prevail over all religion'*, and
>
> {**59.4**} *'That is because they* (the Banu Nadir) *defied God and his Messenger'*, see **⟨45.⟩** above;

and

9. most commonly, to punish unbelievers for their disbelief, including

> {**3.141**} *'So that God may assay those who believe and blight the unbelievers'*,

> {**4.102**} *'Surely God has prepared for the unbelievers a humiliating punishment'*,

> {**4.141**} *'God will not grant the disbelievers a way over the believers'*,

> {**9.26**} above,

> {**9.123**} *'Fight those disbelievers who are close to you...'*,

> and

> {**66.9**} *'O prophet, strive against the unbelievers and the hypocrites and be harsh with them'*.

The belief that the Qur'an represents a single coherent revelation from God requires Muslims to strive to reconcile the verses instructing forbearance in the face of provocation, those that instruct violence until peace is offered, and those that seem motivated by acquisition, revenge, conquest or dominance.

One approach is to treat later verses as having abrogated earlier verses. In the light of the traditional Islamic narrative this means, in effect, that the Qur'an's instructions became more belligerent as Mohammed's power grew – see **Part V The Life of Mohammed** above.

Another approach would be to strictly limit the instructions to violent jihad to the particular circumstances believed to have been faced by Mohammed at the time that the verses were announced and which they were presumably announced to address (see also

Part V but also the problems to this approach outlined in ⟨*15. Mohammed as 'a beautiful example'*⟩.)

A third approach, and one often held by traditionalists, is that a believer may regard military jihad as legitimate and obligatory, but only if it follows certain conditions, namely that it is a territorial conflict fought from an Islamic domain ('*dar al-Islam*' / the '*house of Islam*') against a non-Muslim land ('*dar al-harb*' / the '*house of war*') and directed by a caliph, sultan, emir or a similar religiously authoritative figure (such as does not exist in the present time[55]).

The thirteenth century Taqi ad Deen ibn Taymiyyah drew a distinction between offensive jihad, which requires the leadership of an Islamic ruler, and defensive jihad which does not. Groups of modern volunteer jihadis often construct highly contrived arguments to justify their actions as defensive, in order to come within ibn Taymiyyah's justification.

In other instances, they have gone to some pains to establish a territorial campaign waged from Islamic against non-Islamic territory, seen most recently with the declaration of the Islamic State 'caliphate' (2014-19).[56]

However, these conditions for engaging in jihad, that are attributed to the early jurist Abu Hanifa, are not made explicit in the Qur'an. Since the eighteenth century, many autonomous 'Islamist' groups have formed that have carried out violent non-territorial (terrorist) campaigns that are clearly motivated by one or more of the eight reasons for jihad listed above, in the terms that they are expressed in the Qur'an and, their members can often fairly claim, in imitation of the recorded life of Mohammed.

93. Martyrdom
Surah 61 (al-Saff/The Ranks): 12

10. O You who believe! Shall I guide you to a commerce that will save you from a painful torment?

11. That you believe in Allah and His Messenger (Muhammad, blessings of God be upon him), and that you strive hard and fight in the Cause of Allah with your wealth and your lives, that will be better for you, if you but know!

12. (If you do so) He will forgive you your sins, and admit you into Gardens under which rivers flow, and pleasant dwelling in Gardens of Eden:

Eternity, that is indeed the great success.

[*Hilali & Khan, see* ⟨**14.**⟩]

The traditional Islamic interpretation of {**61.12**} is that whilst most people will be raised and judged by God on the Last Day, ⟨**96.**⟩, those who are martyred in the cause of jihad, called '*shahid*', will have their sins instantly forgiven them and will gain immediate entry to Paradise. See also {**2.245**, **4.74**} and {**9.111**}. These verses may help to explain the appeal of suicide and certain death missions to modern jihadis, especially those who have undergone adult conversion to Islam or an intensification of their faith after having previously lived 'unislamic' lives. For such people, martyrdom offers, on the face of the Qur'an, the only absolute guarantee of avoiding the Hellfire for their past sins.

See also ⟨**97. Judgment**⟩ below.

94. Rules of war

Surah 2 (*al Baqarah/The Cow*): 190

And fight in the way of Allah those who fight you, and transgress not.

Verily Allah loveth not the transgressors.

[Daryabadi, see ⟨56.⟩]

The context of this verse has been given above, see ⟨**38. *The First Permission to Fight*⟩**. Concerning the '*transgressions*' that {**2.190**} instructs Muslims to avoid, Ibn Kathir, author of the most widely used Qur'an commentary, approvingly cites Al Hasan al-Basri[57] who lists them as follows:

- ❖ *mutilating the dead,*

- ❖ *theft (from the captured goods),*

- ❖ *killing women, children and old people who do not participate in warfare,*

- ❖ *killing priests and residents of houses of worship,*

- ❖ *burning down trees and killing animals without real benefit.'*

It will be noted that the above list of transgressions does not prohibit the killing of male prisoners, see ⟨**42. *Captives of Badr*⟩** above, nor the rape and enslavement of the women and children of their enemies, see ⟨**66.**⟩ and ⟨**67.**⟩. {**9.36**} may be intended to limit even these rules of war to just four 'sacred' months in the year.

95. Terms of surrender

Surah 47 (*Muhammad*): 4

When you meet those who disbelieve,
strike at their necks. Then when you have
overwhelmed them, tighten the bonds.

Then free them graciously or hold them for
ransom till war lays down its burden.

Thus (shall it be). And if God willed, He
would take vengeance upon them, but that
He may test some of you by means of
others.

And for those who are slain in the way of
God he will not make their deeds go astray.

[The Study Quran, see ⟨1.⟩]

The traditional rules governing the making of treaties by Muslim commanders are:

❖ that they must call upon their enemy to convert to Islam, and if their enemy agrees to do this they must be left with their possessions,

❖ where the enemy is a People of the Book they should be offered the option to accept their submission to Islamic rule by paying jizya, and

❖ if neither of the above apply, Muslim commanders must, if practicable, fight to kill or enslave their enemy.[58]

X
The End of Days

96. The Last Day

81 (*al-Takwir/The Enfolding*) 14

1. When the sun shall be darkened,

2. When the stars shall be thrown down,

3. When the mountains shall be set moving,

4. When the pregnant camels shall be neglected,

5. When the savage beasts shall be mustered,

6. When the seas shall be set boiling,

7. When the souls shall be coupled,

8. When the buried infant shall be asked [9.] for what sin she was slain,

10. When the scrolls shall be unrolled,

11. When heaven shall be stripped off,

12. When Hell shall be set blazing,

13. When Paradise shall be brought nigh,

14. Then shall a soul know what it has produced.

[*Arberry, see* ⟨16.⟩]

Very many Qur'an verses refer to *'the Last Day'*, *'the Day of Judgment'*, or simply *'the Day'* or *'the Hour'*.

The Qur'an is generally taken to foretell that these events will be preceded by the return of Jesus *'a portent of the hour'*, {**43.61**} see ⟨23.⟩ above. Hadith accounts, attributed to Mohammed, prophesy the appearance of two other supernatural figures who are referred to as the *masih ad dajjal* (the *'false messiah'* or commonly, adopting biblical terminology, the *'antichrist'*),[59] who will rule the world from Constantinople, and the *mahdi* [60] who will arrive together with Jesus to defeat the *masih ad dajjal* and to drive evil from the world prior to the Last Day. Some describe an apocalyptic war between Muslims and Jews, in which the natural world will aid the latter's annihilation.

> *The Hour will not begin until the Muslims fight the Jews and the Muslims will kill them, until a Jew hides behind a rock or a tree, and the rock or tree will say: O Muslim, O slave of Allah, there is a Jew behind me, come and kill him. Except the gharqad (a thorny tree), for it is one of the trees of the Jews.*[61]

For most Shia Muslims, the Mahdi is identified with the 'twelfth imam', Muḥammad ibn al-Ḥasan al Askari, who is believed to have disappeared from human view c. 940.

In the Qur'an, the events of the Last Day shall begin with the breaking free of Gog and Magog, see ⟨30.⟩ above. The visible signs for man will include the shaking of the earth {**19.90**, **27.88**, **56.4-6**, **69.14**, **73.14**, **89.21**, **99.1**}, and in the heavens: *'the sky bringing forth manifest smoke covering the people'* {**44.10-11**} and *'the sun and the moon joining together'* {**75.9**}. God shall then take the earth and heavens in His right hand {**39.67**} and *'roll up the sky like the rolling of scrolls for writing'* {**21.104**}.

At the blowing of a trumpet, ⟨4.⟩, the bodies of those who have died will be resurrected {**23.100**} and {**39.68**}, even if they have turned to stone or iron {**17.50**}; mountains will pass away {**18.47**} *'like clouds'* {**27.88**} or *carded wool'* {**101.5**}, creating a great plain {**84.3-4**} - the Plain of Qiyamah - upon which all men and animals {**6.38**, **81.5**} will, having first been scattered like moths or locusts {**101.4**}, be gathered together for judgment.

97. Judgment

Surah 99 (*al-Zalzalah/The Earthquake*): 6

4. That Day she [*the earth*] shall convey her chronicles [5.] for the Lord inspired her.

6. That Day mankind shall issue forth upon diverse paths to witness their deeds.

7. So whosoever does a mote's weight of good we shall see it, [8.] and whosoever does a mote's weight of evil we shall see it.

[*The Study Quran, see* ⟨1.⟩]

At judgement, God '*shall raise up a witness from every community*' {**4.41**, **16.85**, **28.85**, **33.45**, **57.19**}. Jesus will act as witness for all the People of the Book {**4.159**}: '*There is not one of the People of the Book, but will surely believe in* (Jesus) *before his death, and on the Day of Resurrection he will be a witness against them*'. Mohammed shall be a witness for the community those that believe in him {**2.143**, **22.78**}.

The Qur'an states that throughout a person's life their deeds are meticulously recorded by angels in books {**54.52-53**}, the angel on one's right recording virtuous deeds, the angel on one's left, sins, see ⟨4.⟩ above. At judgment each person shall be handed the record of their deeds as a book in either their right or left hand, indicating the preponderance of good or evil in their deeds and the sentence that they shall receive {**69.19-29**}. {**83.6**} states that '*the book of the profligate*' is kept in Sijjin (literally '*a prison*'), sometimes said to lie deep in the depths of the earth.

Those being judged will not be permitted to speak, {**16.85**, **30.57**, **45.35**}. Instead, those being damned will stand helpless as '*their tongues, their hands and their feet*' {**24.24**}, or in {**41.19-24**} '*their ears,* *their eyes and their skins', 'shall give witness against them for that which they used to do.'* In any event, any speech would be futile since, as God in one well known verse ominously warns:

50.16:

We did indeed create man, and We know what his soul whispers to him, and We are nearer to him than his jugular vein.

There is no consensus in Islam as to the criteria for salvation. Throughout the Qur'an the promise of heaven and threat of hell are frequently directed towards *'believers'* and *'unbelievers'* respectively, for example:

10.103:

We save our messengers and those who believe. Thus, is it incumbent upon Us to save believers.

3.131:

And be mindful of the Fire that has been prepared for the disbelievers.

However, many other verses, such as {99.7-8} above, describe a balancing of deeds, so that each person will judged such that *'every soul is held in pledge for what it has earned'* {52.21} and {74.38}; similarly {13.33}, a judgment according to works rather than faith alone.

The Qur'an, several times, refers to *'those who believe and do good works'* {4.124, 5.9, 16.97, 42.26, 103.3} as though both faith and a preponderance of good works over evil are required for salvation, although in {49.14}, see ⟨90.⟩ above, God appears to offer some reduced measure of salvation for submission even without actual faith.

Moreover, several verses state that believers may be *'absolved from their evil deeds'*, see {5.65, 8.29, 29.7, 47.2}, see ⟨12.⟩ above, {48.5, 64.9} and {65.5}, implying a process of redemption of sins based upon repentance:

66.8:

O you who believe! Repent unto God with sincere repentance.

It may be that your Lord will absolve you of your evil deeds and cause you to enter the Gardens with rivers running below – the Day when God will not disgrace the Prophet and those who believe with him, with their light spreading before them and on their right, while they say 'Our Lord complete our light for us and forgive us.

Thou are Powerful over all things.'

Yet God's forgiveness in the Qur'an is expressed as being more sparingly granted than is the case in the gospels:

4.17:

God only accepts the repentance of those who do evil in ignorance and then turn quickly in repentance

These are the ones unto whom God relents and God is Knowing, Wise.

and, in order to emphasise God's absolute power, His forgiveness is always couched as a residual discretion rather than a promise: God *'forgives whomsoever He will and punishes whomsoever he will'* {**48.14**}, also {**2.105**, **2.284**, **3.129**, **5.18**, **48.14**}.

All of these verses lead to an obvious scope for disagreement within Islam over whether salvation is gained by faith, works, both faith and works together or submission, and in what circumstances one might hope that justice will be tempered with mercy. To add a further complication, yet other verses state that God Himself *'leads some astray'* {**4.88**, **4.143**, **40.74**, **42.44-6**}, *'causes some to err'* {**11.34**} or *'seals their hearts, blinds their eyes and deafens them to the truth'* {**2.7**} which have historically caused many Muslim theologians to adopt a predestinarian outlook.

The words of {**4.31**} *'If you shun the grave sins that you are forbidden, we shall absolve you of our evil deeds and cause you to enter at a noble gate'* seems reassuring, but leaves uncertainty as to what, in God's judgment, may constitute *'the grave sins'*. Given the graphic descriptions of Paradise and the Hellfire, see **(99.)** and **(100.)** below, this issue is a matter of supreme importance to believing Muslims.

The only certainty in Quranic soteriology would seem to be that the shaheed, those who die whilst fighting jihad, will have all their sins forgiven and be admitted to Paradise at the moment of their death, see **(93. *Martyrdom*)** above.

98 The Heights

Surah 7 (*al-A'raf/The Heights*): 46

45. The inhabitants of the Garden will call out to the inhabitants of the Fire 'We have found that which our Lord promised us to be true. Have you found that which your Lord promised to be true?

They will respond 'Yes'.

Thereupon a herald shall proclaim in their midst 'The curse of God be upon the wrongdoers'.

46. And there shall be a veil between them And upon the heights are men who know all by their marks. They will call out to the inhabitants of the Garden 'Peace be upon you'.

They will not have entered it, though they hope.

47. And when their eyes turn towards the inhabitants of the Fire, they will say 'Our Lord, place us not among the wrongdoing people'.

Surah 7 (*The Heights*) takes its name from an area of high ground that will serve as a division between Heaven and Hell. This place will be occupied, it is generally assumed, by those whose evil and good deeds are equally balanced, or possibly by Muslims who have committed no major sins but who have been negligent in performing their religious obligations, or possibly those lacking moral responsibility such as the very young or mentally ill.

The inhabitants still hope to enter Paradise, but fear the Hellfire, both of which are visible to them. These verses suggest that their state of limbo may be temporary, but whether it is so for all, the purpose of any waiting period and the individuals' eventual destination are all left ambiguous.

A popular Islamic image that emerges from the hadith of the route to Paradise after death, is that of the Bridge of Sirat, that is said to be *as thin as a hair and as sharp as a sword*, and which must be traversed in order to reach the Gardens.[62]

> *'It is a slippery (bridge) on which there are hooks like a thorny plant that is wide at one side and narrow at the other and has thorns with bent ends ....*
>
> *Some of the believers will cross the bridge as quickly as the wink of an eye, some others as quick as lightning, a strong wind, fast horses or she-camels.*
>
> *So some will be safe without any harm; some will be safe after receiving some scratches, and some will fall down into Hell.*
>
> *The last person will cross by being dragged over the bridge.'*[63]

99. Gardens of Paradise

Surah 37 (*al-Saffat/Those Arranged in Ranks*): 48

40. Except the chosen (faithful) devotees of
Allah, [41.] there shall be a known provision,
[42.] fruits, and they shall be honored
[43.] in the Gardens of Delight (Paradise),
[44.] on the thrones facing one another,
[45.] served around (them) with a cup of pure
wine, [46.] crystal-white, delicious to the
drinkers.

47. Neither they will have any kind of hurt,
headache or sin in that, nor will they suffer
intoxication from that.

**48. With them will be chaste females
restraining their glances (for husbands
only) with wide and beautiful eyes,**
[49.] as if they were delicate eggs closely
guarded.

[Abdul Hye, see 37.]

Paradise (*Jannah*) in the Qur'an is described variously as one
garden, or two, four or an unspecified number of gardens, and
sometimes vineyards, often '*with streams running beneath*'. The
Gardens are mentioned in a majority of the Quran's surahs, and
described in particular detail in {**37.48**}, above, {**38:52**, **44.54**, **52.17-
27**, **55.56-78**, **56.11-40**} and {**78.31-37**}. They are specifically
identified as being the same Paradise from whence Adam and his
wife, were expelled at the start of the human story, see **(6. Adam)**
above.

The Gardens are presented as an abode of sensual pleasure. Fowl, fruit, milk and honey are each mentioned as provided to eat. Believers will be reunited with believing spouses and family members {13.23, 25.74, 52.20-21}. All shall be waited upon by *'immortal youths'* who will serve them drink from a flowing stream that causes *'neither stupefaction nor headache'* {56.17}.

Famously, men shall have available to them *houris*, who are supernatural *'maidens of modest gaze'*, of like age to the believer, *'wide eyed'*, *'with eyes like concealed pearls'* or *'hidden eggs'* and *'of swelling breasts'* (for Sarwar *'with pear-shaped breasts'* {55.56}; to Ibn Manzur *'young girls whose breasts are beginning to appear'*[64]). In {55.56} these delightful creatures are described as those *'whom neither man nor jinn has ever touched'*, and in {56.35-38} the pleasure that they are created to give is unambiguously erotic:

> 35. Truly we brought (resurrected believers)
> into being as a new creation, [36.] then made
> for them virgins, amorous peers, [38.] for the
> companions of the right.

In {44.54} they are described as available for men to marry.

Subsequent Islamic commentators have speculated that *houris* are completely hairless, transparent, created without the need to urinate, defecate or menstruate, and that they remain virgins despite repeated intercourse.[65] No number of *houris* is ever given in the Qur'an, the popular belief that martyrs will receive seventy-two being based upon a hadith.[66]

In **Surah 55** a four-garden scheme is laid out with one pair of gardens, described in verses {55.48-60}, as more enticing in every way than the other pair in {55.62-76}. In the former gardens, water seems more plentiful (*'flowing'* rather than *'bubbling up'*), there is a wider range of fruit to eat, inhabitants recline on brocade-lined couches rather than sitting on cushions on a carpet, and the houris are described as being *'like ruby and coral stone'* and of *'modest gaze'* as opposed to *'secluded in pavilions'* – possibly indicating greater chastity. Which class of believers gain access to the superior rather than the standard gardens is not made clear.

100. The Hellfire

Surah 22 (*al-Hajj/The Pilgrimage*): 19

**These two adversaries have become
engrossed in contention about their Lord.**

**For the unbelievers garments of fire shall be
cut out, and scalding water will he poured
over their heads**, [20] melting all that is in
their bellies and their skin.

21. In addition, there will be whips of iron for
them.

22. Whenever, in their anguish, they try to
get out, they are returned there, and will be
told: 'Taste the torment of fire!'

[*Sayyid Qutb, see* ⟨*30.*⟩]

Hell (called '*jahannan*', a Hebrew term for hell used by Jesus in the
gospels) is described as an endless excruciating torment, almost
always associated with fire or boiling liquid. Further particularly
gruesome descriptions are found at {**4.55-7**, **14.49-50**, **36.63-7**, **40.70-
72**, **56.90-94**} and {**67.7**}.

As unbelievers burn, fettered and yoked, clad in '*garments made of
pitch*', {**14.50**}, or fire, {**22.19**} above '*as often as their skins are
consumed, We shall replace them with other skins that they may taste the
punishment*', {**4.56**}.

Their only food shall be '*a vile thorn*' {**88.6-7**} the fruit of the *zaqum*
tree that '*emerges in the depth of the hellfire*' {**37.66-7**} and '*oozing pus*'
{**14.16**} (which may be the same substance as '*ghislin*' in {**69.36**} the

translation of which is uncertain); their only drink shall be a boiling liquid that *'tears apart their bowels'* {**47.15**}.

With the descriptions of Hell, as with the descriptions of Heaven, see ⟨**99.**⟩ above, the attention to such practical matters as what inhabitants shall wear and consume, serves to emphasis that the descriptions are intended to be taken literally - and to horrify or tempt accordingly.

There are degrees of Hell. Of these:

> #### 4.145:
>
> Surely the hypocrites will be in the lowest depths of the Fire, and thou wilt not find for them any helper.

Verses of the Qur'an referred to in this book

Surah 1 (*al-Fatihah/The Opening*)

1-7   **Prologue: the bismillah**
                 33. The Salat

Surah 2 (*al-Baqarah / The Cow*)

7   **97. Judgment**, God *'seals hearts'* etc
11   **73.-74. *'Working corruption on the earth'*, use**
                 of *'hirabah'*
23   **8. The Qur'an**, challenge to write verses of
                 similar quality
31-38   **6. Adam**, creation of
                 7. Iblis and al-Shaitan, refusal to prostrate
                 to Adam
41   **17. People of the Book**, the Qur'an
                 confirming earlier revelation
43   **83. Generosity**
48   **1. God**, no intercession
52-53   **7. Iblis and al-Shaitan**
62   **17. People of the Book**, Sabians
65   **87. Unbelievers *'the worst of creatures'*,**
                 God curses some Jews: *'Be ye apes'*
67-72   **21. Moses**, story of the yellow/red cow,
                 25. Apocryphal sources
83   **83. Generosity**
87   **2. God's Spirit**, the Holy Spirit
89, 91   **17. People of the Book**, the Qur'an
                 confirming earlier revelation
97-101   **9. Gabriel,**
                 17. People of the Book, the Qur'an
                 confirming earlier revelation
102   **4. Angels**, Harut and Marut
105   **97. Judgment,** *'God shows mercy to whom He*
                 will'
106   **11. Abrogation**
109   **85. *'Repel evil with good'***
115   **1. God**, anthropomorphism (face)
123   **1. God,** no intercession

Surah 3 (*al Imran/The House of Imran*

Surah 4 (*al Nisa*/*Women*)

1	**6. Adam,** humanity created from a single soul, creation of a mate
3	**59. Polygamy**
11-12	**65. Inheritance**
13	**14. Obedience to Mohammed,** '*Obey God and His Messenger*'
15	**68. Fornication/Adultery,** sentence of confinement till death
16	**70. Homosexuality,** '*two amongst you*'
17	**97. Judgment,** conditions for forgiveness
22-23	**59. Eligibility for marriage,** *mahram* relationships
24	**67. Intercourse with** '*those one's right hand possesses*'
25	**68. Fornication/Adultery,** sentence halved for slaves
29	**92. Honesty,** honesty in commerce
31	**97. Judgment,** minor and grave sins
34	**61. Beating one's wife for disobedience**
36	**83. Generosity**
41	**97. Judgment,** a witness from every community
43	**72. Consuming alcohol and gambling,** not attending prayers drunk
48	**1. God,** the sin of shirk unforgivable
55-57	**100. The Hellfire,** replacement of skins
58	**92. Honesty,** honouring trust
59	**14. Obedience to Mohammed,** '*Obey God and His Messenger*'
65	**14. Obedience to Mohammed,** Mohammed as judge
69	**14. Obedience to Mohammed,** '*Obey God and His Messenger*'
74	**93. Martyrdom,** immediate entry to Paradise
74-76	**92. Reasons for jihad,** to capture Mecca
77	**57. Zakat,** essential to recognition as believer
82	**8. The Qur'an,** challenge to write verses of similar quality

Surah 5 (*al Ma'idah/ The Table Spread*)

3	**77. Dietary rules,** **13.** *'Islam'*
4	**59. Eligibility for marriage,** women of the Book
9	**97. Judgment,** *'those who believe and do good works'*
12-19	**17. The People of the Book,** condemned, **83. Generosity** **85.** *'Repel evil with good'* **97. Judgment,** God *'forgives whom He will'*
15	**8. The Qur'an,** clear
17	**23. Jesus,** Messiah, not the son of God
27-32	**A. Biblical Figures in the Qur'an,** Cain & Abel
31	**25. Apocryphal sources,** Cain and the raven
32-33	**73.-74.** *'Working corruption on the earth'*
38	**71. Theft,** sentence of amputation
41-86	**17. The People of the Book,** condemned
43	**17. People of the Book,** reference to the Torah
45	**75. Qisas**
48	**17. People of the Book,** the Qur'an confirming earlier revelation **85.** *'Repel evil with good'*
51-52	**88.** *'Al-wala wal bara'*, *'Take not unbelievers as allies'*, re Jews and Christians
54	**91. Meaning of jihad,** jihadis lauded, **88.** *'Al-wala wal bara'*, double standard between believers/unbelievers
57	**88.** *'Al-wala wal bara'*, *'Take not unbelievers as allies'*
59-60	**88. Unbelievers** *'the worst of creatures'*, God turns People of the Book to apes, swine.
65	**97. Judgment,** absolution
66-68	**17. People of the Book,** Torah and Injeel
69	**17. People of the Book,** Sabians
72	**23. Jesus,** 'Messiah'

Surah 6 (al-Anam/The Cattle)

Surah 7 (*al-Araf/the Heights*)

Surah 8 (*al-Anfal/The Spoils of War*)

1-17	**41. The Battle of Badr**, before the battle
	91. Meaning of Jihad, exhortation to fight
	92. Reasons for jihad, to demonstrate God's power, to punish disbelief, to further Islamic rule
27	**92. Honesty**, honouring trust
29	**97. Judgment**, absolution
30	**1. God**, *'the best of plotters'*
39-48	**41. The Battle of Badr**, reviewed,
	92. Reasons for jihad, to further Islamic rule
55-57	**92. Reasons for jihad**, to demonstrate God's power
	87. Unbelievers *'the worst of creatures'*
59	**92. Reasons for jihad**, to punish disbelief
65	**91. Meaning of Jihad**, exhortation to fight
67	**42. Treatment of the captives of Badr**,
	92. Reasons for jihad, to demonstrate God's power
72-73	**88. 'Al-wala wal bara'**, *'Take not unbelievers as allies'*
74	**91. Meaning of jihad**, jihadis lauded
148	**92. Reasons for jihad**, to reward Muslims with spoils of war

Surah 9 (*al-Tawbah/Repentence*)

5	**52. 'The Sword Verse'**,
	57. Zakat, essential to recognition as believer,
	91. Meaning of Jihad, exhortation to fight
11	**57. Zakat**, essential to recognition as believer
12	**92. Reasons for jihad**, retribution, to remove an obstacle to the practice of Islam
19	**31. Mecca and Yathrib**, *'al Masjid al Haram'*;
	91. Meaning of Jihad, contrast with helping pilgrims

Surah 10 (*Jonah*)

Surah 11 (*Hud*)

7	**3. Creation**, in six days
13	**8. The Qur'an**, challenge to write verses of similar quality
25-49	**18. Noah**
34	**97. Judgment**, God *'causes some to err'*
50-60	**27. Arab prophets**, Hud
61-68	**27. Arab prophets,** Saleh
69-76	**19. Abraham**, visit from angels
84-94	**27. Arab prophets**, Shuaib, **92. Honesty**, false measures by the people of Midian,
114	**33. Salat,** three prayer times

Surah 12 (*Joseph*)

All	**A. Biblical figures in the Qur'an**, Joseph
1	**8. The Qur'an,** clear
2	**8. The Qur'an**, sent down in Arabic
26-28	**25. Apocryphal sources**, Joseph's torn tunic
67	**25. Apocryphal sources**, Entering Pharaoh's court

Surah 13 (*al-Ra'd/The Thunder*)

2	**1. God**, anthropomorphism (throne)
16	**88. '*Al-wala wal bara*'**, *'Take not unbelievers as allies'*
22	**85. '*Repel evil with good'***
23	**99. Gardens of Paradise**, reunion with family
33	**97. Judgment,** weighing good and evil deeds
39	**8. The Qur'an**, the *'mother of the book'*

Surah 14 (*Abraham*)

Surah 15 (*al-Hijr*)

Surah 16 (*al-Nahl/The Bee*)

Surah 17 (*al-Isra/The Night Journey*)

Surah 18 (*al-Kahf/The Cave*)

Surah 19 (*Mary*)

2-11	**9. Gabriel,** announcing the forthcoming birth of John the Baptist
16-21	**2. God's Spirit,** appears as a perfect man
	23. Jesus, born of a virgin
24	**25. Apocryphal sources,** Jesus's miracles of the palm tree and the spring
28	**24. Bible/Qur'an Discrepancies**
30-38	**23. Jesus,** words, prediction of death, not the son of God
	83. Generosity
42-52	**19. Abraham,** rebellion against father
55	**83. Generosity**
56	**A. Biblical Figures in the Qur'an,** Idris
88	**1. God,** has not taken a child
90	**96. The Last Day,** signs of (earth shaking)
97	**8. The Qur'an,** *'easy upon the tongue'*

Surah 20 (*Ta Ha*)

5	**1. God,** anthropomorphism (throne)
11-24	**21. Moses,** talking to God
37-40	**1. God,** anthropomorphism (eye),
	21. Moses, raised as an orphan
43-60	**21. Moses,** preaching
53	**3. Creation,** earth *'spread out'*
109	**1. God,** possible intercession
115-123	**6. Adam,**
	7. Iblis and al-Shaitan, temptation of Adam and Eve
130	**33. Salat,** two prayer times and night prayer

Surah 21 (*al-Anbiya-The Prophets*)

28	**1. God,** possible intercession
30-33	**3. Creation,** of the heavens and the earth
73	**83. Generosity**

Surah 22 (*al-Hajj/The Pilgrimage*)

Surah 23 (*al-Mu'minun/The Believers*)

24 (*al-Nur/Light*)

2	**68. Fornication/Adultery**, sentence of flogging,
	55. Rules for Mohammed's wives, sentence doubled for Mohammed's wives
4	**69. ...Unsupported allegations**
11-24	**7. Iblis and al-Shaitan**, '*follow not the footsteps of*',
	69. ... Unsupported allegations,
	97. Judgment, body parts to bear witness
26, 27	**84. Respect for others**, not entering a house without permission
31	**80. Modest female attire**
33	**66. Slavery**, freeing a slave for payment
51	**14. Obedience to Mohammed**, Mohammed as judge
55	**92. Reasons for jihad**, to further Islamic rule
58	**33. Salat,** two prayer times
61	**77. Dietary rules**, permitted eating places etc
63	**14. Obedience to Mohammed**

Surah 25 (*al-Furqan/The Criterion*)

54	**6. Adam**, humanity created from water
59	**1. God**, anthropomorphism (throne)
	3. Creation, in six days
63	**85. '*Repel evil with good*'**, 'saying '*Peace*'
74	**99. Gardens of Paradise**, reunion with family

Surah 26 (*al-Shu'ara/The Poets*)

52-56	**21. Moses**, leading Israelites into wilderness
69-82	**19. Abraham**, rebellion against his father
105-122	**18. Noah**
123-139	**27. Arab prophets**, Hud
141-158	**27. Arab prophets**, Saleh

Surah 27 (*al-Naml/The Ants*)

Surah 28 (*al-Qasas/The Story*)

Surah 29 (*al-Ankabut/The Spider*)

Surah 30 (*The Byzantines*)

2-5	**86. Believers and unbelievers**, believers rejoicing at Byzantine resurgence
17-18	**33. Salat,** four prayer times
20	**6. Adam**, humanity created from dust
38	**1. God**, anthropomorphism (face)
	83. Generosity, list of recipients
39	**58. Usury**
57	**97. Judgment**, people not permitted to speak

Surah 31 (*Luqman*)

4	**83. Generosity**
12-19	**27. Arab prophets**, Luqman,
	23. Jesus, parable of the mustard seed
28	**6. Adam**, humanity created from a single soul

Surah 32 (*Fatir/The Originator*)

4	**1. God**, anthropomorphism (throne), no intercession
9	**2. God's Spirit**, breathed into Adam
11	**4. Angels**, the angel of death

Surah 33 (*al-Ahzab/The Parties*)

4-5	**64. Adoption**
10	**46. Battle of the Trench**
13	**31. Mecca and Yathrib**, Yathrib named
21	**15. Mohammed** *'a beautiful example'*
25	**92. Reasons for jihad**, to punish disbelief
26-27	**47 ... The Banu Qurayza**,
	92. Reasons for jihad, to reward Muslims with spoils of war

Surah 34 (*Saba/Sheba*)

Surah 35 (*al-Sajdah/Prostration*)

Surah 36 (*Ya-Sin*)

38	**30. Dhu'l Qarnayn**, the sun's dwelling place
39	**3. Creation**, path of moon like a dried palm
60	**7. Iblis and al-Shaitan**
63-67	**100. The Hellfire**

Surah 37 (*al-Saffat/Those Arranged in Ranks*)

6-10	**3. Creation**, shooting stars;
	7. Iblis and al-Shaitan, shaitans (plural)
11	**6. Adam**, humanity created from clay
41-49	**99. Gardens of Paradise**, incl. houris
67	**100. The Hellfire**, the zaqum tree
83-96	**19. Abraham**, rebellion against father
102	**20. Isaac and Ishmael**, Eid al Adha
123-132	**A. Biblical Figures in the Qur'an**, Elias
138-148	**A. Biblical Figures in the Qur'an**, Jonah
149	**1. God**, has no daughters (angels)
150-154	**4. Angels**, not female

Surah 38 (*Sad*)

13	**27. Arab prophets**, Shuaib
17-29	**A. Biblical Figures in the Qur'an**, David
30-40	**22. Solomon**, corpse on throne
41-44	**A. Biblical Figures in the Qur'an**, Job
52	**99. Gardens of Paradise**, incl. houris
72	**2. God's Spirit**, breathed into Adam
74-75	**1. God**, anthropomorphism (hands);
	6. Adam,
	7. Iblis and al-Shaitan, refusal to prostrate to Adam

Surah 39 (*al-Zumar/The Throngs*)

6	**6. Adam**, humanity created from a single soul, creation of a mate
22	**13.** *'Islam'*
44	**1. God**, no intercession
67	**1. God**, anthropomorphism (right hand)
	96. The Last Day, God takes heaven and earth in His right hand
68	**4. Angels**, Raphael,
	96. The Last Day, resurrection of the dead

Surah 40 (*Ghafir/The Forgiver*)

7	**1. God**, intercession from angels
15	**2. God's Spirit**, bringing down God's command
55	**33. Salat,** two prayer times
70-72	**100. The Hellfire**
74	**97. Judgment**, God *'leads some astray'*

Surah 41 (*Fussilat/Expounded*)

3	**8. The Qur'an**, sent down in Arabic
7	**57. Zakat**, failure to pay equivalent to disbelief
9-12	**3. Creation**, of the heavens and the earth, in eight days
19-24	**97. Judgment**, body parts to bear witness
34	**85.** *'Repel evil with good'*
36	**7. Iblis and al-Shaitan**, *'seek refuge in God'*
42	**10. The reliability of the recitation**

Surah 42 (*al-Shura/Counsel*)

7	**31. Mecca and Yathrib**, *'Mother of all Cities'*
26	**97. Judgment**, *'those who believe and do good works'*
40	**85. 'Repel evil with good'**, *'pardon and set matters aright'*
44-46	**97. Judgment**, God *'leads some astray'*
52	**2. God's Spirit**, bringing down God's command

Surah 43 (*al-Zukhruf/The Gold Ornaments*)

4	**8. the Qur'an**, the *'mother of the book'*
10	**3. Creation**, earth *'spread out'*
16	**1. God**, has no daughters (angels)
46-56	**21. Moses**, preaching
57-61	**23. Jesus**, not the son of God, return at the Last Day
80	**4. Angels**, recording man's deeds
89	**85. 'Repel evil with good'**, 'saying '*Peace*'

Surah 44 (*al-Dukhan/Smoke*)

2	**8. The Qur'an**, the Night of Ppower
10-11	**96. The Last Day**, signs of (smoke in sky)
17-31	**21. Moses**, preaching, leading Israelites into wilderness
54	**99. Gardens of Paradise**, incl. houris
58	**8. The Qur'an**, *'easy upon the tongue'*

Surah 45 (*al-Jathiyah/Upon Their Knees*)

3-5	**3. Creation**, of the heavens and the earth
35	**97. Judgment**, people not permitted to speak

Surah 46 (*al-Ahqaf/The Sand Dunes*)

Surah 47 (*Muhammad*)

Surah 48 (*al-Fath/The Victory*)

Surah 49 (*al-Hujarat/The Private Apartments*)

Surah 54 (*al-Qamar/The Moon*)

1-2	**37. Splitting the moon**
9-17	**1. God**, anthropomorphism (eyes)
	8. The Qur'an, easy to remember,
	18. Noah
8-21	**27. Arab prophets**, Hud
22	**8. The Qur'an**, easy to remember
32	**8. The Qur'an**, easy to remember
40	**8. The Qur'an**, easy to remember
45-47	**41. The Battle of Badr**, before the battle
52	**97. Judgment**
71	**18. Noah**

Surah 55 (*al-Rahman/The Compassionate*)

8-9	**82. Honesty**, false measures
14	**6. Adam**, humanity created from clay
15	**5. Jinn**, created from fire
27	**1. God**, anthropomorphism (face)
33	**5. Jinn**, Qur'an addressed to
48-78	**99. Gardens of Paradise**, four-Garden
56	(two levels of luxury) scheme for Paradis
	5. Jinn, sexuality

Surah 56 (*al-Waqi'ah/The Event*)

4-6	**96. The Last Day**, signs of (earth shaking)
11-40	**99. Gardens of Paradise**, incl. houris
77-80	**8. The Qur'an**, a 'Preserved Tablet'
90-94	**100. The Hellfire**

Surah 57 (*al-Hadd/Iron*)

4	**1. God**, anthropomorphism (throne),
	3. Creation, of the heavens and the earth

Surah 64 (*al-Taghabun/Mutual Dispossession*)

9	**97. Judgment**, absolution

Surah 65 (*al-Talaq/Divorce*)

4	**59. Eligibility for marriage**, marriageable age
5	**97. Judgment**, absolution
12	**3. Creation**, of the heavens and the earth, seven heavens and the earth '*likewise*'

Surah 66 (*al-Tahrim/Forbiddance*)

1-5	**55. Rules for Mohammed's wives**, Mohammed not bound by word, threat to replace wives with ones more obedient
	9. Gabriel
8	**97. Judgment**, absolution
9	**92. Reasons for jihad**, to punish disbelief
12	**2. God's Spirit**, breathed into Mary

Surah 67 (*al-Mulk/Sovereignty*)

3-5	**3. Creation**, seven heavens, shooting stars
7	**100. The Hellfire**

Surah 68 (*al-Qalam/The Pen*)

4.	**15. Mohammed '*a beautiful example*'**, Mohammed's '*exalted character*'
42	**1. God**, anthropomorphism (shin)
48-50	**A. Biblical Figures in the Qur'an**, Jonah

Surah 69 (*al-Haqqah/the Undeniable Reality*)

14	**96. The Last Day**, signs of (earth shaking)
19-29	**97. Judgment**, people given the book of their deeds
36	**100. The Hellfire**, eating '*ghislin*'

Surah 70 (*al-Ma'arij/The Ascending Ways*)

4	**2. God's Spirit**, distinguished from angels
30	**67. Intercourse with** '*those one's right hand possesses*'
32	**82. Honesty**, honouring trust

Surah 71 (*Noah*)

1-28	**3. Creation**, of the heavens and the earth seven heavens, moon and sun are lights, **18. Noah**

Surah 72 (*al-Jinn/The Jinn*)

8-9	**3. Creation**, shooting stars
11	**5. Jinn**

Surah 73 (*al-Muzzammil/The Enwrapped One*)

14	**96. The Last Day**, signs of (earth shaking)

Surah 74 (*al-Muddaththir/The Covered One*)

38	**97. Judgment**, weighing good and evil deeds
48	**1. God**, no intercession

Surah 75 (*al-Qiyamah/The Resurrection*)

9	**96. The Last Day**, sun and moon joining

Surah 76 (*al-Insan/Man*)

9	**1. God,** anthropomorphism (face)

Surah 78 (*al-Naba/The Tiding*)

7	**3. Creation**, mountains as 'stakes'
31-37	**99. Gardens of Paradise**, incl. houris
38	**2. God's Spirit**, distinguished from angels

Surah 80 (*Abasa/He Frowned*)

11-16	**8. The Qur'an,** a *'Preserved Tablet'*

Surah 81 (*al-Takwir/The Enfolding*)

1-14	**96. The Last Day**, signs of

Surah 82 (*al-Infitar/The Cleaving Asunder*)

10-12	**4. Angels**, recording man's deeds

Surah 83 (*al-Mutaffifin/Those who Defraud*)

1-7	**82. Honesty**, false measures
	97. Judgment, Sijjin

Surah 84 (*al-Inshiqaq/The Sundering*)

3-4	**96. The Last Day**, the plain of Qiyamay

Surah 85 (*al-Buruj/The Constellations*)

All	**27. The elephant**, the People of the Ditch

Surah 86 (*al-Tariq/It comes by night*)

6-7	**79. Women are '*a tilth*'**

Surah 88 (*al-Ghashiyah/The Overwhelming Event*)

6-7	**100. The Hellfire**, the zaqum tree
22	**8. The Qur'an,** a '*Preserved Tablet*'

Surah 89 (*al-Fajr/The Dawn*)

21	**96. The Last Day**, signs of (earth shaking)

Surah 90 (*al-Balad/The Land*)

13	**66. Slavery**, freeing a slave as an act of piety

Surah 96 (*al-Alaq/The Blood Clot*)

1-5 **6. Adam**, humanity created from a clot of
blood
32. The first revelation

Surah 97 (*al-Qadr/Power*)

All **8. the Qur'an**, the Night of Power
4 **2. God's Spirit**, bringing down God's
command, distinguished from angels

Surah 98 (*al-Bayyinah/The Clear Proof*)

6 **87. Unbelievers '*the worst of creatures*'**,
'*the worst of creation*'

Surah 99 (*al-Zalzalah/The Earthquake*)

1 **96. The Last Day**, signs of (earth shaking)
4-8 **97. Judgment**, weighing good and evil deeds

Surah 101 (*al-Qariah/The Calamity*)

4-5 **96. The Last Day**, the plain of Qiyamay

Surah 103 (*al-Asr/The Declining Day*)

3 **97. Judgment**, '*those who believe and do good
works*'

Surah 105 (*al-Fil/ The Elephant*)

All   **27. The elephant**

Surah 109 (*al-Kafirun/ The Disbelievers*)

1-6   **35.** *'To you your religion and to me mine'*

Surah 111 (*al-Masad/The Palm Fibre*)

1-5   **34. Mohammed's family**, Abu Lahab

Surah 112 (*al-Iklas/Sincerity*)

1-4   **1. God**, has not taken a child
                     23. Jesus, not the son of God.

Notes

[1] *The Qur'an, A Historical-Critical Introduction*, 2017, Sinai

[2] *Questioning Islam*, 2014, Townsend

[3] Sahih al-Bukhari 3.50.894, 8.75.419, 9.93.489; Sahih Muslim 6475-6; Jami al-Tirmidhi 3506, 3508 and Sunan ibn Majah 3860.

[3] Sahih Bukhari 8.75.419 and 9.93.483

[4] *Gott hat die schönsten Namen … Islamische Gottesnamen, ihre Bedeutung, Verwendung und Probleme ihrer Übersetzung* [*God Has the most Beautiful Names. God's Names in Islam, their Meaning, Use, and Problems with their Translation*], 2009, Molla-Djafari

[5] Sahih Muslim 7134

[6] Sahih Muslim, 2814

[7] This is a major source for the better known *Mohammed's Koran*, 2017, McLoughlin & Robinson

[8] *The Syro-Aramaic reading of the Quran*, 2011, Luxenberg

[9] *The Hidden Origins of Islam*, ed. Ohlig & Puin: *The Early History of Islam, following inscriptional and numismatic testimony*, Popp; *Early Islam A critical reconstruction based on contemporary sources*, ed. Ohlig: *From Muhammad Jesus to Prophet of the Arabs, a Christological Epiphet,* Ohlig.

[10] Abraham youth stories appear in the *Book of Jubilees* (c.150 BC) and the *Apocalypse of Abraham* (c.AD 70-150).

[11] Including Ibn Kathir, author of the most widely consulted Qur'an commentary.

[12] As recorded by Ibn Ishaq, paragraph 1 of the Guillaume rendering.

[13] *The Bible and the Quran*, 2018, Reynolds

[14] Sahih Bukhari, 1.1.3, also 4.55.605

[15] See *the Priest and the Prophet*, 2005, Joseph Azzi; also *Jewish Christianity and the Origins of Islam*, 2015

[16] '*It is easier for a camel to pass through the eye of a needle than for a rich man to enter the kingdom of heaven*'

[17] As recorded by Ibn Ishaq, paragraphs 29-41.

[18] In *The Antiquities of the Jews* II, 6

[19] In *Hagarism*, 1977, and *Meccan Trade and the Rise of Islam*, 1987, Patricia Crone sets out to demonstrate that Mecca could not have formed part of any major trade route – an essential part of the traditional Islamic narrative. In *Quranic Geography* (2015) Dan Gibson produced detailed measurements to show that the earliest mosques all pointed towards Petra in Jordan rather than Mecca and points out that Petra matches all the descriptions of the location of Mecca in the traditional accounts of Mohammed's life. Such claims became known to a wider audience by Tom Holland's 2012 *In The Shadow of the Sword*, and television documentary the following year, *Islam The Untold Story*.

[20] *The Qur'an, A Historical-Critical Introduction*, 2017, Sinai

[21] Winkler, 1928, cited in *Understanding the Qur'an Themes and Style*, 2011, Haleem

[22] In *Studies in Islamic History and Traditions* by S D Goitein (2010) observes that Psalm 54/55 refers to three daily prayers that has become customary in Judaism, and Psalm 118/119 to seven, which was the basis of the Christian monastic liturgy of the hours and suggests that Islam developed a '*middle way*' between the two.

[23] Sahih Bukhari 4.56.831

[24] Sahih Bukhari 5.58.208

[25] *Quranic Geography*, 2015, Gibson

[26] Ibn Ishaq, paragraph 689

[27] Ibn Ishaq, paragraphs 684-693

[28] *Muhammad, Islam's First Great General*, 2007, Gabriel, page 144

[29] Sahih Bukhari 60.311

30 Sahih Muslim 1474 (honey); Tafsir al-Tabari 66.1 (intercourse with Maryam)

31 Sunan al-Sughra of al-Narsa'i 5004

32 (Re: dolls) Sahih al-Bukhari 8.73.151; (re: ages) al-Bukhari 5.58.234,236; 7.62.64, 65 and 88; Sunan Abu Dawood 4915

33 Jami at-Tirmidhi 1128 and Sunna ibn Majah 1953.

34 Per Haleem, page 55.

35 Sahih Bukhari 7.62.132, and 8.73.68 and Abu Dawood 2137, 2138 and 2139. Abu Dawood (2142) recounts that Mohammed ruled: '*A man shall not be asked why he beat his wife*'.

36 Sahih al-Bukhari 3.4.56.6 and 7, 7.64.266; Sahih Muslim 3996 and 4000, and Sunna ibn Majah 2711

37 From just the two '*sahih*' (most trusted) collections: Sahih al-Bukhari 2.23.413, 3.34.421, 3.49.860, 3.50.885, 4.56.829, 6.60.79, 7.63.195, 196 and 230, 8.78.629, 8.82.803, 805, 806, 809, 810, 813, 816 and 842, 9.89.303, 9.92.432, 9.93.633 and Sahih Muslim 4191, 4194, 4196, 4198, 4199, 4201, 4202, 4205-4207, 4209, 4211, 4212, 4216, 4483. Jami al-Tirmidhi 1431; also the Musnad of Ahmad Hanbal, 157, assert that Umar considered writing the verse into the Qur'an so convinced was he that Mohammed's practise should be recorded as God's will.

38 Sahih al-Bukhari 6.60.70

39 It was narrated that Aishah said: '*The verse of stoning and of breastfeeding an adult ten times was revealed, and the paper was with me under my pillow. When the Messenger of Allah died, we were preoccupied with his death, and a tame sheep came in and ate it.* ' Sunan Ibn Majah 1944, a tradition also reported in the Musnad of Ahmad Hanbal.

40 Sahih al-Bukhari 3.48.829.

41 Sunan Abu Dawood 4447, at-Tirmidhi 152 and Sunan ibn Majah 2561.

42 Sahih al-Bukhari 8.81.774, 780-782

[43] Mohammed is reported as having ordered flogging for the first one or two offences of being intoxicated but death for a *'third or fourth'* offence; but then to have relented and ordered flogging to remain the sentence, even for repeat offenders, *per* Sunan Abu Dawood 4470. In Sahih al-Bukhari (8.81.768, 771 and 772) Mohammed is said to have ordered a habitual drunkard whose nickname was Donkey to be flogged but warned his companions not to curse him as despite his failings he still loved Allah.

[44] The incident is recorded in no less than seventeen hadith including: Sahih Bukhari 1.4.242, 5.59.505, 7.71.623, 8.82.794 and 797; and Sahih Muslim 4131.

[45] Exodus: 21.24-25, Leviticus 24.20 and Deuteronomy 19.16-21.

[46] Jami al-Tirmidhi 1399. See also Sunan ibn Majah 2662.

[47] Sahih al-Bukhari 6.60.115 and Sunan Abu Dawood 3963.

[48] Sunan Ibn Majah 1926, Al Adad Al Mufrad (6.120). The term is also included in Abu Hanifa's *Kitab al Athar* (443), the earliest book of Sharia judgments.

[49] In fact saying he would have put the man's eye out with his comb had he seen him, Sunan al-Sughra of al-Narsa'i 5.54.154

[50] From 537 to 752 the Byzantine Empire exercised effective control over the papacy. The Great Schism between Catholic and Orthodox churches occurred in 1054.

[51] Per *The Study Quran*

[52] Sahih al-Bukhari 3.47.789 and 792, 4.53.407 and 8.73.9; Sahih Muslim 2194-5 and Sunan Abu Dawood 1664.

[53] First recorded in *The History of Baghdad,* by al-Khatib al-Baghdadi (1002-1071).

[54] The traditional understanding of the 'town' from whence people cry to be saved in **4.75**. (eg Ibn Kathir)

[55] The last caliphate with any widespread credibility in the Islamic world was the Ottoman caliphate, that came to an end in 1923.

[56] Other examples include the Wahhabi-Saudi desert war that led to the establishment of the Kingdom of Saudi Arabia and various

campaigns against the Sikh Kingdom and the British Raj waged in what is now Afghanistan/Pakistan in the eighteenth and nineteenth centuries: see *God's Terrorists*, 2017, Allen.

[57] *The Reliance of the Traveller*, 1368, a Sha'afi law text, 9.8-15.

[58] Ibid.

[59] Sahih al-Bukhari 3.30.106, 9.88.241, 246 and 248, 9.93.565; Sahih Muslim 7005, 7017, 7019 and 7034.

[60] Sunna ibn Majah 4083 and 4086; Jami al Trimidhi 2232 and Sunan Abu Dawood 4271-2.

[61] Sahih Muslim 2922, also 2921; Sahih al-Bukhari 4.56.791.

[62] Sahih al-Bukhari 1.12.770

[63] Sahih al-Bukhari 9.93.532

[64] Cited in *Understanding the Qur'an, Themes and Style*, 2011, Abdel Haleem

[65] Sahih al-Bukhari 55.544

[66] Jami al-Trimidhi, approved by Ibn Kathir, which states that '*The smallest reward for the people of Heaven is an abode where there are eighty thousand servants and seventy-two houri, over which stands a dome decorated with pearls, aquamarine, and ruby, as wide as the distance from al-Jabiyyah to San'a.*'

Printed in Great Britain
by Amazon